Orphan Factory

POETS ON POETRY

David Lehman, General Editor
Donald Hall, Founding Editor

New titles

Josephine Jacobsen, *The Instant of Knowing*
Charles Simic, *Orphan Factory*
William Stafford, *Crossing Unmarked Snow*
May Swenson, *Made with Words*

Recently published

A. R. Ammons, *Set in Motion*
Douglas Crase, *AMERIFIL.TXT*
Suzanne Gardinier, *A World That Will Hold All the People*
Allen Grossman, *The Long Schoolroom*
Jonathan Holden, *Guns and Boyhood in America*
Andrew Hudgins, *The Glass Anvil*
Kenneth Koch, *The Art of Poetry*
Martin Lammon (editor), *Written in Water, Written in Stone*
Carol Muske, *Women and Poetry*

Also available are collections by

Robert Bly, Philip Booth, Marianne Boruch, Hayden Carruth,
Fred Chappell, Amy Clampitt, Tom Clark, Robert Creeley,
Donald Davie, Peter Davison, Tess Gallagher, Thom Gunn,
John Haines, Donald Hall, Joy Harjo, Robert Hayden,
Daniel Hoffman, Weldon Kees, Galway Kinnell, Mary Kinzie,
Richard Kostelanetz, Maxine Kumin, David Lehman,
Philip Levine, John Logan, William Matthews, William Meredith,
Jane Miller, John Frederick Nims, Gregory Orr, Alicia Ostriker,
Marge Piercy, Anne Sexton, Charles Simic, Louis Simpson,
William Stafford, Richard Tillinghast, Diane Wakoski,
Alan Williamson, Charles Wright, and James Wright

Charles Simic

Orphan Factory

ESSAYS AND MEMOIRS

Ann Arbor
THE UNIVERSITY OF MICHIGAN PRESS

A CIP catalog record for this book is available from the British Library.

Library of Congress Cataloging-in-Publication Data

Simic, Charles, 1938–
Orphan factory : essays and memoirs / Charles Simic.
p.   cm. — (Poets on poetry)
Includes bibliographical references.
ISBN 0-472-09663-X. — ISBN 0-472-06663-3 (pbk.)
1. Simic, Charles, 1938–   —Authorship.   2. Poets, American—20th
century—Biography.   3. Poetry—Authorship.   I. Title   II. Series.
PS3569.I4725Z472   1997
811′.54—dc21   97-23678
                                                           CIP

Contents

New York Days, 1958–1964

Even the old Romans knew. To have a son for a poet is bad news. I took precautions. I left home when I was eighteen. For the next couple of years I lived in a basement apartment next to a furnace that hissed and groaned as if it were about to explode any moment. I kept the windows open in all kinds of weather, figuring that way I'd be able to crawl out on the sidewalk in a hurry. All winter long I wrote bad poems and painted bad pictures, wearing a heavy overcoat and gloves in that underground hole.

At the Chicago newspaper where I worked, I proofread obituaries and want ads. At night, I dreamed of lost dogs and funerals. Every payday I put a little money aside. One day I had enough to quit my job and take a trip to Paris, but I treated my friends to a smorgasbord in a fancy Swedish restaurant instead. It wasn't what we expected: there was too much smoked fish and pickled herring. After I paid the bill, everybody was still hungry, so we went down the street for pizza.

My friends wanted to know: When are you going to Paris? "I've changed my mind," I announced, ordering another round of beers. "I'm moving to New York, since I no longer have the money for Paris." The women were disappointed, but the fellows applauded. It didn't make sense, me going back to Europe after only being in the States for four years. Plus, to whom in Paris would I show my poems written in English?

"Your poems are just crazy images strung arbitrarily together," my pals complained, and I'd argue back: "Haven't you heard about surrealism and free association?" Bob Burleigh, my best

From an excerpt of a memoir in progress that was first published in the *Gettysburg Review* 9, no. 3 (1996): 373–535.

friend, had a degree in English from the University of Chicago and possessed all the critical tools to do a close analysis of any poem. His verdict was: "Your poems don't mean anything."

My official reply to him was: "As long as they sound good, I'll keep them." Still, in private, I worried. I knew my poems were about something, but what was it? I couldn't define that "something" no matter how hard I tried. Bob and I would often quarrel about literature until the sun came up. To show him I was capable of writing differently, I wrote a thirty-page poem about the Spanish Inquisition. In the manner of Pound in his *Cantos,* I generously quoted original descriptions of tortures and public burnings. It wasn't surrealism, everybody agreed, but you still couldn't make heads or tails of what was going on. In one section, I engaged Tomás de Torquemada in a philosophical discussion, just like Dostoyevsky's Ivan did with the Grand Inquisitor. I read the poem to a woman called Linda in a greasy spoon on Clark Street. When we ran to catch a bus, I left the poem behind. The next morning, the short-order cook and I tried to find it buried under the garbage out back. But it was a hot summer day, and the trash in the alley smelled bad and was thickly covered with flies. So we didn't look too closely.

Later, I stood at the corner where we caught the bus the night before. I smoked a lot of cigarettes. I scratched my head. Several buses stopped, but I didn't get on any of them. The drivers would wait for me to make up my mind, then give me a dirty look and drive off with a burst of speed and a parting cough of black smoke.

I left Chicago in August 1958 and went to New York, wearing a tan summer suit and a blue Hawaiian shirt. The weather was hot and humid. The movie marquees on Forty-second Street were lit up twenty-four hours a day. Sailors were everywhere, and a few mounted policemen. I bought a long cigar and lit it nonchalantly for the benefit of a couple of young girls who stood at the curb afraid to cross the busy avenue.

A wino staggered up to me in Bryant Park and said: "I bark back at the dogs." A male hooker pulled a small statue of Jesus out of his tight pants and showed it to me. In Chinatown I saw a white hen pick a card with my fortune while dancing on a hot grill. In Central Park the early morning grass was matted where unknown lovers lay. In my hotel room I kept the mirror busy by making stranger and stranger faces at myself.

"Sweetheart," a husky woman's voice said to me when I answered the phone at four in the morning. I hung up immediately.

It was incredibly hot, so I slept naked. My only window was open, but there was a brick wall a few feet outside of it and no draft. I suspected there were rats on that wall, but I had no choice.

Late mornings, I sat in a little luncheonette on Eighth Street reading the sport pages or writing poems:

> In New York on 14th Street
> Where peddlers hawk their wares
> And cops look the other way,
> There you meet the eternal—
> Con artists selling watches, silk ties, umbrellas,
> After nightfall
> When the crosstown wind blows cold
> And my landlady throws a skinny chicken
> In the pot to boil. Fumes rise.
> I can draw her ugly face on the kitchen window,
> Then take a quick peek at the street below.

It was still summer. On advice of my mother, I went to visit an old friend of hers. She served me tea and cucumber sandwiches and asked about my plans for the future. I replied that I had no idea. I could see that she was surprised. To encourage me, she told me about someone who knew at the age of ten that he wanted to be a doctor and was now studying at a prestigious medical school. I agreed to come to a dinner party where I would meet a number of brilliant young men and women my age and profit by their example. Of course, I failed to show up.

At the Phoenix Book Shop in the Village, I bought a book of French stories. It was on sale and very cheap, but even so I only had enough money left to buy myself a cup of coffee and a toasted English muffin. I took my time sipping the lukewarm coffee and nibbling my muffin as I read the book. It was a dark and rainy night. I walked the near-empty streets for hours in search of the two people I knew in the city. Not finding them home, I returned to my room, crawled shivering under the covers, and read in the silence, interrupted only by the occasional wailing of an ambulance:

> Monsieur Lantin had met the girl at a party given one evening by his office superior, and love had caught him in its net.
>
> She was the daughter of a country tax-collector who had died a few years before. She had come to Paris then with her mother, who struck up acquaintance with a few middle-class families in her district in the hope of marrying her off. They were poor and decent, quiet and gentle. The girl seemed the perfect example of a virtuous woman to whom every sensible young man dreams of entrusting his life. Her simple beauty had a modest, angelic charm, and the imperceptible smile that always hovered about her lips seemed to be a reflection of her heart.

After midnight my hotel was as quiet as a tomb. I had to play the radio real low with my ear brushing against it in the dark. "Clap your hands, here comes Charlie," some woman sang, a hot Dixieland band backing her up, but just then I didn't think it was very funny.

While the weather was still good, I sat on benches in Washington Square Park or Central Park, watching people and inventing stories to go along with their faces. If I was wearing my only suit and it rained, I sat in the lobbies of big hotels smoking cigars. I went window-shopping almost every night. An attractive pair of shoes or a shirt would make me pay a return visit even after midnight. The movies consumed an immense amount of my time. I would emerge after seeing the double-feature twice, dazed, disoriented, and hungry. I often had a toothache and waited for days for it to go away. I typed with two fingers on an ancient Underwood typewriter that woke my hotel neighbors. They'd knock on my walls until I stopped. On a Monday morning while everyone else was rushing off to work, I took a long subway ride to Far Rockway. Whenever the subway came out of the ground, I would get a glimpse of people working in offices and factories. I could tell they were hot and perspiring. On the beach there were only a few bathers, seemingly miles apart.

When I stretched out on the sand and looked up, the sky was empty and blue.

When I was on the way home late one night, a drunk came out of a dark doorway with a knife in hand. He swayed and couldn't say what he wanted. I ran. Even though I knew there was no chance he would catch up with me, I didn't stop for many blocks. When I finally did, I no longer knew where I was. Around that time, I wrote:

> Purse snatchers
> Keep away from poor old women
> They yell the loudest.
> Stick to young girls,
> The dreamy newlyweds
> Buying heart-shaped pillows for their beds.
> Bump into a drunk instead,
> Offer a pencil to sell.
> When he pulls out a roll of bills,
> Snatch all he's got and split.
> Duck that nightstick
> Or your ears will ring
> Even in your coffin.

I am not exaggerating when I say that I couldn't take a piss without a book in my hand. I read to fall asleep and to wake up. I read at my various jobs, hiding the book among the papers on my desk or in the half-open drawer. I read everything from Plato to Mickey Spillane. Even in my open coffin, some day, I should be holding a book. *The Tibetan Book of the Dead* would be most appropriate, but I'd prefer a sex manual or the poems of Emily Dickinson.

The book that made all the difference to my idea of poetry was an anthology of contemporary Latin-American verse that I bought on Eighth Street. Published by New Directions in 1942 and long out of print by the time I bought my copy, it introduced me to the poems of Jorge Luis Borges, Pablo Neruda, Jorge Carrera Andrade, Drumond de Andrade, Nicholas Guillen, Vincente Huidobro, Jorge de Lima, César Vallejo, Octavio Paz, and so many others. After that anthology, the poetry I read in literary magazines struck me as pretty timid. Nowhere in the

Sewanee Review or the *Hudson Review* could I find poems like "Biography for the Use of the Birds" or "Liturgy of My Legs" or this one, by the Haitian poet, Emile Roumer, "The Peasant Declares His Love":

> High-yellow of my heart, with breasts like tangerines,
> you taste better to me than eggplant stuffed with crab,
> you are the tripe in my pepper-pot,
> the dumpling in my peas, my tea of aromatic herbs.
> You're the corned beef whose customhouse is my heart,
> my mush with syrup that trickles down the throat.
> You're a steaming dish, mushroom cooked with rice,
> crisp potato fried, and little fish fried brown . . .
> My hankering for love follows you wherever you go.
> Your bum is a gorgeous basket brimming with fruits and meat.

The folk surrealism, the mysticism, the eroticism, and the wild flights of romance and rhetoric in these poets were much more appealing to me than what I found among the French and German modernists that I already knew. Of course, I started imitating the South Americans immediately:

> I'm the last offspring of the old raven
> Who fed himself on the flesh of the hanged . . .
> A dark nest full of old misfortunes,
> The wind raging above the burning treetops,
> A cold north wind looking for its bugle.

I was reading Jakob Böhme in the New York Public Library on Forty-second Street on a hot, muggy morning when a woman arrived in what must have been last night's party dress. She was not much older than I, but the hour and the lack of sleep give her a world-weary air. She consulted the catalog, filled out a slip, received her book, and sat down at a table across from mine. I craned my neck, I squinted in my nearsighted way, and I even brushed past her a couple of times, but I could not figure out what she was reading. The book had no pictures, and it wasn't poetry, but she was so absorbed that her hair fell into her eyes. Perhaps she was sleeping.

Then, all of a sudden, when I was absolutely sure she was

snoozing away, she turned a page with a long, thin finger. Her fingers were too thin, in my opinion. Was the poor dear eating properly? Was she dying of consumption? Her breasts in her low-cut black dress, on the other hand, looked pretty healthy. I saw no problem there.

Did she notice my spying on her? Absolutely not, unless she was a consummate actress, a budding Gene Tierney.

Of all the people I watched surreptitiously over the years, how many noticed me and still remember me the way I remember them? I just have to close my eyes, and there she is, still reading her mysterious book. I don't see myself and have no idea what I look like or what clothes I'm wearing. The same goes for everyone else in the large reading room. They have no faces; they do not exist. She's reading slowly and turning pages carefully. The air is heavy and muggy and the ceiling fan doesn't help. It could be a Monday or a Thursday, July or August. I'm not even certain if it was 1958 or 1959.

I went to hear Allen Tate read his poems at New York University. There were no more than twenty of us all together: a few friends of the poet, a couple of English professors, a scattering of graduate students, and one or two oddballs like me seated way in the back. Tate was thin and dapper, polite, and read in what I suppose could be described as a cultivated Southern voice. I had already read some of his essays and liked them very much, but the poetry, because of its seriousness and literary sophistication, was tedious. You would have to be nuts to want to write like that, I thought, remembering Jorge de Lima's poem in which he describes God tattooing the virgin: "Come, let us read the virgin, let us learn the future . . . / O men of little sight." Not a spot on her skin without tattoos: "that is why the virgin is so beautiful," the Brazilian poet says.

On a hot night in a noisy, crowded, smoke-filled jazz club, whiskey and beer were flowing, everyone was reeling with drink. A fat woman laughed so hard, she fell off her chair. It was difficult to hear the music. Someone took a muted trumpet solo I tried to follow with my left ear, while with my right I had to listen to two women talk about a fellow called Mike, who was a scream in his bathing suit.

It was better to go to clubs on weeknights, when the crowd was smaller and there were no tourists. Best of all was walking in after midnight, in time to catch the final set of the night. One night when I arrived, the bass and the drums were already playing, but where was Sonny Rollins, whom I came to hear? Finally we heard a muffled saxophone: Sonny was in the men's room, blowing his head off. Everybody quieted down, and soon enough he came through the door, bobbing his shaved head, dark shades propped on a nose fit for an emperor. He was playing "Get Happy," twisting it inside out, reconstituting it completely, discovering its concealed rhythmic and melodic beauties, and we were right there with him, panting with happiness.

It was great. The lesson I learned was: cultivate controlled anarchy. I found Rollins, Charlie Parker, and Thelonious Monk far better models of what an artist could be than most poets. The same was true of the painters. Going to jazz clubs and galleries made me realize that there was a lot more poetry in America than one could find in the quarterlies.

At one of the readings at NYU given by a now forgotten academic poet of the 1950s, just as the professional lovers of poetry in the audience were already closing their eyes blissfully in anticipation of the poet's familiar, soul-stirring clichés, there was the sound of paper being torn. We all turned around to look. A shabby old man was ripping newspapers into a brown shopping bag. He saw people glare at him and stopped. The moment we turned back to the poet, who went on reading, oblivious of everything, in a slow monotone, the man resumed ripping, but now more cautiously, with long pauses between rips.

And so it went: the audience would turn around with angry faces, he'd stop for a while and then continue while the poet read on and on.

My first job in the city was selling men's dress shirts in Stern's Department store on Forty-second Street. I dressed well and learned how to flash a friendly smile. Even more importantly, I learned how to let myself be humiliated by the customers without putting up the slightest resistance.

My next job was in the Doubleday Bookstore on Fifth Avenue. I would read on the sly while the manager was busy elsewhere. Eventually I could guess what most of the customers wanted even before they opened their mouths. There were the best-seller types and the self-help book types, the old ladies in love with mysteries, and the sensitive young women who were sure to ask for Khalil Gibran's *The Prophet*.

But I didn't like standing around all day, so I got a job typing address labels at New York University Press. After a while they hired another fellow to give me help. We sat in the back room playing chess for hours on end. Occasionally, one of the editors would come and ask us to pick up his dry cleaning, pay an electric bill, buy a sandwich or a watermelon.

Sal and I took our time. We sat in the park and watched the girl students go by. Sal was a few years older than I, and a veteran of the air force. When he was just a teenager, his parents died suddenly and he inherited the family bakery in Brooklyn. He got married and in two years had ruined the business.

How? I wanted to know. "I took my wife to the Latin Quarter and Copacabana every night," he told me with obvious satisfaction. He joined the air force to flee his creditors. Now he was a veteran and a homespun philosopher.

Sal agreed with H. L. Mencken that you are as likely to find an honest politician as you are an honest burglar. Only the church, in his view, was worse: "The priests are all perverts," he confided to me, "and the pope is the biggest pervert of all."

"What about Billy Graham?" I asked, trying not to drop my watermelon.

"That's all he thinks about," Sal assured me with a wink.

The military was no better in his view. All the officers he had met were itching to commit mass murder. Even Ike, in his opinion, had the mug of a killer.

Only women were good. "If you want to have a happy life," he told me every day, "learn to get along with the ladies."

After several fleabag hotels, I finally found a home at Hotel Albert on Tenth Street and University Place. The room was small, and of course the window faced a brick wall, but the location was perfect, and the rent was not too high. From Friday noon to Sunday morning, I had plenty of money. The rest of the week, I scraped by on candy bars for lunch and hamburgers or cheap Chinese food for dinner. Later I would buy a glass of beer for fifteen cents and spend the rest of the night perfecting the art of making it last forever.

My first poems were published in the winter 1959 issue of the *Chicago Review,* but other publications came slowly after that: the mail brought me rejection slips every day. One, I remember, had a personal note from the editor that said: "Dear Mr. Simic, you're obviously an intelligent young man, so why do you waste your time writing so much about pigs and cockroaches?"

To spit on guys like you, I wanted to write back.

After work on Fridays, my friend Jim Brown and I would tour the bars. We'd start with a few beers at the Cedar Tavern, near our rooms, then walk over to the San Remo on MacDougal Street, where Brown would have a martini and I would drink red wine. Afterward, we would most likely go to the White Horse, where Brown had a tab, to drink whiskey. With some of the regulars, Brown would discuss everything from socialism to old movies; I didn't open my mouth much, for the moment I did and people heard my accent, I would have to explain where I came from, and how, and why. I thought of printing a card, the kind deaf panhandlers pass around, with my abbreviated life story on it and an abbreviated account of the geography and history of the Balkans.

Around midnight Brown and I would walk back to Cedar, which was packed by then, and have a nightcap. Over hamburgers, Brown would harangue me for not having read Rabelais or Sir Thomas Browne yet. Later, lying in my bed, with drink and talk floating in my head and the sound of creaking beds, smokers' coughs, and love cries coming from the other rooms, I would not be able to sleep. I would go over the interesting and stupid things I had heard that night.

For instance, there were still true believers around in those days who idealized the life in the Soviet Union and disparaged the United States. What upset me the most was when some nice-looking young woman would nod in agreement. I reproached myself for not telling her how people over there were turned into angels at the point of a gun. My shyness and cowardice annoyed me no end. I couldn't fall asleep for hours and then, just as I was finally drifting off, one of my rotten teeth would begin a little chat with me.

With the arrival of the Beats, both as a literary movement and as a commercial venture, the scene changed. Coffee shops sprang up everywhere in the Village. In addition to folk singing and comedy acts, they offered poetry readings. *Where the Beat Meet the Elite,* said a banner over a tourist trap. "Oh God, come down and fuck me!" some young woman prayed in her poem, to the horror of out-of-town customers.

But New York was also a great place for poetry: within the same week, one could also hear John Berryman and May Swenson, Allen Ginsberg and Denise Levertov, Frank O'Hara and LeRoi Jones. I went to readings for two reasons: to hear the poets and to meet people. I could always find, sitting grumpily in the corner, someone with whom it was worth striking up a conversation. The readings themselves left me with mixed feelings. One minute I would be dying of envy, and the next with boredom and contempt. It took me a few years to sort it all out. In the meantime, I sought other views. I'd spot someone thumbing an issue of the *Black Mountain Review* in the Eighth Street Bookstore and end up talking to them. Often that would lead to a cup of coffee or a beer. No matter how hip you think you are, someone always knows more. The literary scene had a greater number of true originals then than it has today—autodidacts, booze hounds, and near derelicts who were walking encyclopedias—for example Tony, an unemployed bricklayer, who went around saying things like: *Even the mutes are unhappy since they've learned to read lips,* and *It took me sixty years to bend down to a flower.*

Then there was the tall, skinny fellow with graying hair I talked to after hearing Richard Wilbur read at NYU. He told me that the reason contemporary poets were so bad was because they were lazy. I asked what he meant and he explained: "They write a couple of hours per week, and the rest of the time they have a ball living in the lap of luxury with rich floozies hanging on their arms and paying their bills. You've got to write sixteen hours per day to be a great poet." I asked him what he did, and he muttered that he worked in the post office.

During one of my rare trips back to Chicago to visit my mother, Bob Burleigh told me about a terrific young poet I ought to meet. His name was Bill Knott. He worked nights in a hospital emptying bedpans and was usually at home during the day. He lived in a rooming house not too far away, so we went to see him.

An old woman answered the bell and said Bill was upstairs in his room. But when we knocked there was no answer. Bob shouted, "It's me, Bob." Just as we were about to leave, I heard a sound of hundreds of bottles clinking together, and the door opened slowly. Soon we saw what it was: we had to wade through an ankle-deep layer of empty Pepsi bottles to advance into the room. Bill was a large man in a dirty white T-shirt, one lens of his glasses was wrapped with masking tape, presumably broken. The furnishings were a bed with a badly stained mattress, a large poster of Monica Vitti, a refrigerator with an old TV set on it, and a couple of chairs and a table with piles of books on them. Bob sat on the bed, and I was given a chair after Bill swept some books on the floor. Bill, who hadn't sat down, asked us: "How about a Pepsi?" "Sure," we replied. "What the heck!" The fridge, it turned out, contained nothing but rows and rows of Pepsi bottles.

We sipped our sodas and talked poetry. Bill had read everything: we spoke of René Char, and Bill quoted Char from memory. Regarding contemporary American poetry, we were in complete agreement: except for Robert Bly, James Wright, Frank O'Hara, and a few others, the poets we read in the magazines were the most unimaginative, dull, pretentious, know-nothing bunch you were ever likely to encounter. As far as these poets were concerned, Arthur Rimbaud, Hart Crane, and Guillaume Apollinaire might never have existed. They knew nothing of modern art, cinema, jazz. We had total contempt for them. We bought magazines like *Poetry* in those days in order to nourish our rage: Bob and I regularly analyzed its poems so we could grasp the full range of their imbecility. I did not see any of Bill

Knott's poems that day, but later he became one of my favorite poets.

Back in New York, I had a long talk with Robert Lowell about nineteenth-century French poetry. We were at a party following some reading at the Y. It was late, and most people had gone home. Lowell was seated in an armchair, two young women were sitting on the floor, one on each side of him, and I was on the floor facing him. Although he spoke interestingly about Charles Baudelaire, Tristan Corbière, and Jules Laforgue, what had me totally captivated were not his words, but his hands. Early in our conversation, he massaged the women's necks; after a while he slid his hands down inside their dresses and worked their breasts. They didn't seem to mind, hanging on his every word. Why wasn't I a great poet? Instead of joining in, I started disagreeing with him, told him that he was full of shit. True, I had flunked out of school in Paris, but when it came to the French vernacular, my ear could not be faulted. Lowell did not seem to notice my increasing nastiness, but his two groupies certainly did. Finally, I said good-night and split. I walked from the upper West Side down to my room in the Village, fuming and muttering like an old drunk.

Another time I was drinking red wine, chain-smoking, and writing, long past midnight. Suddenly, the poem took off, the words just flowing, in my head a merry-go-around of the most brilliant similes and metaphors. *This is it!* I was convinced there had never been such a moment of inspiration in the whole history of literature. I reread what I'd written and had to quit my desk and walk around the room, I got so excited. No sooner was I finished with one poem than I started another even more incredible one. Toward daybreak, paying no attention to my neighbor's furious banging on the wall, I typed them out with my two fingers and finally passed out exhausted on the bed. In the morning, I dragged myself to work, dead tired but happy.

When evening came, I sat down to savor what I wrote the night before, a glass of wine in my hand. The poems were terrible!

Incoherent babble, surrealist drivel! How could I have written such crap? I was stunned, depressed, and totally confused.

It wasn't the last time this had happened: nights of creative bliss followed by days of gagging. With great clarity I could see every phony move I had made, every borrowing, every awkwardness. Then I found myself in a different kind of rush: I had only seconds left to rip up, burn, and flush down the toilet all these poems before the doctors and nurses rushed in and put me in a straitjacket. Of course, the next night, I was at it again, writing furiously and shaking my head in disbelief at the gorgeous images and metaphors flooding out of my pen.

I have thrown out hundreds of poems in my life, four chapters of a novel, the first act of a play, fifty or so pages of a book on Joseph Cornell. Writing poetry is a supreme pleasure, and so is wiping the slate clean.

Today people sometimes ask me when I decided to become a poet. I never did. The truth is, I had no plans: I was content merely to drift along. My immigrant experience protected me from any quick embrace of a literary and political outlook. Being a suspicious outsider was an asset, I realized at some point. Modernism, which is already a collage of various cultures and traditions, suited me well. The impulse of every young artist and writer to stake everything on a single view and develop a recognizable style was, of course, attractive, but at the same time I knew myself to be pulled in different directions. I loved Whitman and I loved the surrealists. The more widely I read, the less I wanted to restrict myself to a single aesthetic and literary position. I was already many things, so why shouldn't I be the same way in poetry?

One evening I would be in some Village coffee shop arguing about Charles Olson and projective verse, and the next evening I would be eating squid in a Greek restaurant, arguing in Serbian with my father or Uncle Boris about Enrico Caruso and Beniamino Gigli, Mario Del Monaco, and Jussi Bjoerling.

On one such evening, a nice, old, silver-haired lady, pointing to three other silver-haired ladies smiling at us from the next table, asked Boris and me: "Would you, please, tell us what language you are speaking?"

Boris, who never missed an opportunity to play a joke, made a long face, sighed once or twice, and—with moist eyes and a sob in his voice—informed her that, alas, we were the last two remaining members of a white African tribe speaking a now nearly extinct language.

That surprised the hell out of her! She didn't realize, she told us, now visibly confused, that there were native white African tribes.

"The best-kept secret in the world," Boris whispered to her and nodded solemnly while she rushed back to tell her friends.

It was part of being an immigrant and living in many worlds at the same time, some of which were imaginary. After what we had been through, the wildest lies seemed plausible. The poems that I was going to write had to take that into account.

Charles the Obscure

Late one night, as the half-moon rode high above the church of St. Mark, I grabbed my balls while passing a priest. This happened in Belgrade when I was twelve years old. I was skipping along without a care in the world when he came around the corner. He assumed I was about to greet him—he was even inclining his head benevolently—then I did what my friends advised me to do when meeting a priest. He stood there steaming in his cassock for a moment. Then it was my turn to be surprised. Plump as he was, he went after me with extraordinary quickness, waving his arms about and shouting: "You little creep! You little son of a bitch!" His cussing terrified me even more than the chase he gave me. I ran without looking back.

At home the photographs of my great-great-grandfathers and uncles awaited me on the living room walls. On my mother's side, I had several priests and one bishop in my ancestry. I've never seen a wanted poster with a more murderous collection of mugs. They had huge black-and-white beards that grew even sideways. Their eyes were bulging. The photographer must have warned them not to move, and they obeyed. Flies crawled inside of their ears during the long exposure. Their noses itched terribly. That evening, after the priest, their eyes followed me with unusual grimness. They all knew what I had done.

The meanest looking of the lot was my grandfather's father. It was public knowledge that his children hated him. My grandfather did not permit any mention of priests or religion in our house when he was around. When my grandmother died, he

From *New Letters* 60, no. 4 (1994), written for the special issue on poetry and religion.

informed the family that there would be no priest officiating in the cemetery chapel or at the gravesite. A scandal, people whispered. Everybody crossed themselves just thinking about it. A couple of aunts decided to disobey his wishes. The priest would appear at the gravesite while the coffin was being lowered; and my grandfather, so the theory went, would be too overwhelmed with grief and sorrow to object to a short prayer being said.

That's not what happened. Just as the gravediggers were fussing with the ropes, and the family and friends were standing with bowed heads, the priest materialized in his vestments, a prayer book in hand, already blessing us and mumbling a prayer. To everyone's astonishment, grandpa lunged at him. Before we had time to realize what was happening, the old curmudgeon had the priest by the scruff of the neck and was marching him away from the grave. As if that wasn't enough, one of my weeping aunts ran after them, grabbed the tails of grandfather's coat and started pulling him back. She had the strength of ten, and so did he. A tug of war ensued and lots of yelling. The old man was trying to kick her without turning and letting the priest go. Unfortunately, my mother rushed me and my brother away before we could see and hear more.

If you had asked anybody in my family if God exists, they would have given you a puzzled look. Of course he does, they would have replied. This meant, in practice, attending the church only to baptize, wed, and bury someone. Bona fide atheists probably mention religion and God more frequently than my mother ever did. My father, however, was a different story. He didn't mind entering churches. Russian churches, black churches, old Italian churches, austere New England churches, Byzantine churches, all were admirable. The same is true of me. He liked the pomp and music, but he liked an empty church even more. A few times I saw him get down on his knees to pray, but he had no use for organized religion, or for any other idea that has sought to take its place. As far as he was concerned, communism and fascism were versions of the nastiest aspects of Christianity. "All that orthodoxy, fanaticism, virtue by decree," he'd complain. They were all enemies of the individual, forever peddling intolerance and conformity. He had serious philosophical interest in Islam,

Buddhism, Hinduism, and Christianity, but no desire to join any congregation of the faithful. Belief in God was something private, like sex. If you did not believe in anything, as I often told him was the case with me, that was all right, too.

"Come on," she yanked my arm. "Let's go. They're just a couple of hicks," she assured me, but I had to take a better look at the street preachers.

The young woman with thick glasses pressed a Bible to her heart; the horse-faced fellow by her side strummed a tuneless guitar at the edge of a large Saturday night crowd. They preached and sang hymns as if dogs were biting their asses.

My friend had had enough. Without my noticing, she split. I was left in custody of their Jesus, who, by the sound of it, had too many lost sheep already to worry about. His great love always spurned—"Sweet Jesus," they hollered, trying to drown out an ambulance crying its heart out somewhere in the dark city beyond the brightly lit movie houses and penny arcades all around us.

Hell! I was deeply moved.

America is God crazy, as everyone knows. It's impossible to be an American writer without taking that into account.

Driving just after daybreak early one spring morning through West Virginia, I'm listening to the radio. Someone is playing scratchy old black gospel records. The station is fading and coming clear in turn; the car is speeding down the empty road, and I'm wondering who is choosing the records so impeccably, so mysteriously, given the odd hour. Beyond the enjoyment, the emotion is gripping me, I have a sudden realization: They mean every word they say. Every word. They sing so beautifully, and so wildly, because they believe the Lord is in their midst right then and there.

It has always seemed obvious to me that we are alone in the universe. I love metaphysics and its speculations, but the suspicion at the core of my being is that we are whistling in the dark. Still, I have tears in my eyes every time I hear good church music. Never has the human heart been so pure, I think. Perhaps divinity can only be experienced by those who sing together? The God who comes or does not come to the solitaries is a different one.

"Without this mystery, the most incomprehensible of all, we are incomprehensible to ourselves," said Pascal, in a different context.

Sing and shout, Reverend! is my advice. Do that little dance step while the choir behind you sways and slaps its tambourines, and the old lady on the piano and the scrawny kid on the electric guitar nod to each other with approval. There's no doubt about it: "Except for music, everything is a lie," as Cioran says.

One day I finally admitted to myself that I'm hopelessly superstitious. You do not believe in God, I said to myself, so how come you believe in bad luck? I have no reply to that. Do we make our Fate, or is our Fate an independent agency? Calvin at least knew who arranged our destiny; I do not.

This head full of contradictions walking on two legs, is this the modern version of holy foolishness? Let's hope so.

In the meantime, the worries of a crumb overlooked on death's dinner plate . . .

I was always attracted to mystical and esoteric doctrines that propose the unknowingness of the Supreme Being, the ineffability of the experience of his presence and the ambiguity of our human condition. Ambiguity, that great carnivore. If I believe in anything, it is in the dark night of the soul. Awe is my religion, and mystery is its church. I include here equally the mysteries of consciousness and the torments of conscience.

If not for conscience would we ever consider the possibility of the independent existence of evil? Nothing explains the world and the people in it. This is the knowledge that makes us fall down on our knees and listen to the silence of the night. Not even a dog or an owl is brave enough to interrupt it tonight. Being and nothingness, those two abstractions, how real, how close they feel. In such moments I want to reach for my chessboard. Let them play each other, and I'll sit and watch until the first streak of light slips under the door and crawls to my feet without waking the dust.

Many years ago, Vasko Popa took me to visit the women's monastery Mesic, near his hometown, Vršac, on the Yugoslav-Rumanian border. We had a long lunch at a young poet's house and did not leave till five in the afternoon. I don't remember much about the drive, since we were talking a lot, interrupting each other with stories and jokes; but all of a sudden there was a high wall at the end of a dirt road and a closed iron gate. We left the car outside the gate and pushed it open just enough to squeeze through. What we found inside was a veritable jungle, as if the grass had not been cut all summer, and the trees had grown wild over the years without being trimmed and thinned out. We followed what was once a road, and now a narrow path in the twilight calm broken occasionally by the sound of a bird or cricket. We did not speak. After a mile or so, we saw through the trees several large houses and a small Byzantine church. We walked to the largest of them, knocked, opened the door, peeked inside, even announced ourselves; but only silence came out to welcome us. It was so quiet, our steps became cautious. We walked on tiptoe on the way to the next house. Through the open door, we could see six nuns sitting in a circle with heads bowed. Vasko knew the name of the prioress and called out to her. She jumped, and the nuns followed after her in joy and delight to see him. The prioress, who was old, used to be in her youth a lady in waiting at the royal court, Vasko had told me, and was exceptionally well educated. Vasko sent her French books. She was just reading Camus and immediately wanted to talk about him with us.

We were then given a tour by the prioress and a tall, skinny young nun. We visited the church, which was under repair, to see some surprisingly fine frescoes, and then slowly, because of the prioress's age, we climbed to the small graveyard above the church. The sun had just set. "I'll be soon resting here," the prioress told us, laughing. We smiled in reply. One could almost envy the prospect.

Then we were led back to the large house we had first come to. This we heard was one of the local bishop's many summer residences. He had not stayed in it for the last thirty years, but everything was kept in readiness for his arrival. We sat in a large living room with the prioress and the skinny nun drinking homemade brandy, while being sternly examined by former bishops in sooty old paintings. Only one table lamp had been lit. Vasko talked and so did the old woman, but the rustling of so many leaves muffled their voices, and then all of a sudden, there was complete silence. Here was peace of a world outside time, the kind one encounters at times in fairy-tale illustrations, in which a solitary child is seen entering a dark forest of gigantic trees.

After a while I listened only to the silence deepen, the night continue to hold its breath.

"Every poem, knowingly, or unknowingly, is addressed to God," the poet Frank Samperi told me long ago. I remember being surprised, objecting, mentioning some awful contemporary poems. We were filing subscription cards in the stock room of a photography magazine and having long philosophical conversations on the subject of poetry. Frank had been reading a lot of Dante, so I figured, that's it. He is stuck in fourteenth-century Italy.

No more. Today I think as he did then. It makes absolutely no difference whether gods and devils exist or not. The secret ambition of every true poem is to ask about them even as it acknowledges their absence.

Orphan Factory

Experts in the manufacture of orphans.

—Anna Akhmatova

The last time I talked to my mother, the day before she died at the age of eighty-nine in the winter of 1994, she asked me:

"Are those idiots still killing each other?"

I told her yes, and she sighed and rolled her eyes with exasperation. She had stopped watching television and reading the papers, but she had a pretty good idea what sort of dirty little war they were having in Yugoslavia. Every time I came to visit her in the nursing home, she'd ask me the same question, and I would give her the same answer. Despite being well educated and widely traveled, my mother had no understanding of the world. Wars, even those fought, supposedly, for the worthiest of causes, made no sense to her.

What about the Nazis, my brother and I would ask her. Surely those bastards were worth fighting?

She'd shrug her shoulders and wave us away. No heroes for her. Idiots killing idiots was how she saw it. When my brother was in Vietnam, she wrote a letter to President Johnson telling him that he had no business sending young people to die over there. She even called him a lousy liar and a murderer of children. I was sure she'd get a visit from the FBI. Instead, she received a two-line form letter from the White House informing her that the president appreciated her interesting views.

From *Frankfurter Allgemeine Zeitung,* August 24, 1995.

"They are cutting someone's throat in Pera's cornfield." My young aunt ran into the house shouting at the top of her lungs.

"May I go and see?" I asked my mother, which made my aunt shriek even louder at the horror of it all. She didn't stop until they slapped her face and put her to bed.

I don't recollect that event well, but I have a clear memory of the view of the cornfield from our bedroom window. The corn in August 1944 was already high. At times I saw crows hover over it and dive quickly, but mostly the sky was empty and blue. Still, for days after, they would not let me come near that window, even though its heavy curtains were drawn as if it were wintertime.

Today when I watch the war in Yugoslavia on TV, I have the feeling I'm watching the reruns of my childhood. It's like the networks were all engaged in some far-out science fiction plot to pluck the images out of my head. The bombed buildings, the corpses lying in the streets of Sarajevo, the crowds of refugees are all frighteningly familiar.

My own home movie begins with the German bombing of Belgrade on April 6, 1941, when a bomb hit the building across the street. I flew out of my bed all the way across the room. I was three years old and more astonished than I actually was frightened by the flames that rose everywhere.

"How come these bombs hardly ever hit anything of military importance?" I asked the poet Richard Hugo, who had bombed me in Belgrade on a regular basis in 1944 for the American air force. He was terribly upset that he had bumped into someone, and someone he liked, who had actually been the recipient of his bombs, but I assured him that I bore no grudges. You, Yankees, were our dear allies, I explained to him. We were happy to be pounded by you. I just wanted to know the reason why all the important buildings and the old Gestapo headquarters were still standing and the poorest neighborhoods were in ruins?

What Hugo told me made sense. Their primary mission was the oil fields in Romania, which were heavily defended. They often lost a plane. On the way back to Italy, they were supposed to unload the remaining bombs over Belgrade. Of course, they took no chances. They flew high and dropped their loads in the general direction of the city. Understandably, they were in a big hurry to get back, kiss the ground, and thank the Lord for being alive, before rushing off to the beach with some nice Italian girl. As for murdering innocent folk, that's more or less what everybody expects everybody to do in a war.

Then, as now, in Yugoslavia, there was a nasty civil war in progress. It was not enough for us natives that the country was occupied by Germans, Italians, Bulgarians, and even Hungarians who were all no slouches when it came to murdering the innocent. We, the victims, spent four years trying to outdo our occupiers in cruelty. In the little town near Belgrade where my grandfather had a house and we went to take a breather from the bombings of the city, the main local pastime was murder. Mihailovic's Chetnik's were killing commies and the commies were killing Chetniks. In addition, we had the followers of the fascist General Ljotic; we had the collaborators of General Nedic; we had the White Russian troops who fought on the German side; and we had assorted other psychopaths who worked alone or in groups. We even had a couple of Italian soldiers who were disarmed and abandoned after the fall of Mussolini. They went knocking on people's doors and asking the kind signora for something to eat in exchange for doing any odd jobs. They were the only soldiers among the lot I liked and trusted.

Around dinner table every night the talk turned to the day's horrors: The shoemaker and his family had their throats cut last night. The high school teacher of French was arrested. The Sava river was full of fresh corpses floating down from Croatia. There were four dead men lying in the ditch on the road to some village.

This wasn't just unfounded rumor. Running around the countryside, my friends and I saw plenty of corpses in the last months of war. I never went near them. The few who were bolder and did, tried to frighten the rest of us with gory details. All this seemed unsurpassably awful, until I heard the stories of what went on in Bosnia, Herzegovina, Krajina, and Montenegro. Horror, like anything else people do, has its degrees. I realized early on that my wartime experiences were comparatively idyllic. We always had the city to run back to, and the city despite the bombs has ways of protecting one that a small village in the wilds of Bosnia or Herzegovina just cannot do.

"I only regret not having had an opportunity to kill my father," a Montenegrin intellectual told me years later in New York. He had the face and a manner one would ordinarily describe as sensitive, so his words came as a great shock to me. The members of his family, as was often the case, took different sides in the civil war, and his father was on the wrong side. In him, and in so many others I encountered after the war, I sensed a hatred so huge, so vicious and mindless that any attempt to counter it with pleas for forgiveness and reasonableness was met with total incomprehension, and their hatred turning eventually against me. For my mother, the murderers of all nations belonged to a single nation, the nation of murderers, a view that I always found eminently sensible and regrettably in the minority. Still, I guess, if you know that your sister and mother were killed and raped by a Serb or a Croat, it's hard to confine your hatred to just that one Serb or Croat. Loathing and cries for vengeance do not distinguish between individual and collective responsibility.

The marching music of the next century will undoubtedly be religion and nationalism. The choir practice has already started. Children of light and children of darkness are already being sorted out everywhere. Brutality, violence, and inhumanity, as Simon Weil knew, have always had an immense and secret prestige. We now only require a new superior morality to justify them.

All that became obvious to me watching the dismemberment of Yugoslavia, the way opportunists of every stripe over there instantly fell behind some vile nationalist program. Yugoslav identity was enthusiastically canceled overnight by local nationalists and Western democracies in tandem. Religion and ethnicity were to be the main qualifications for citizenship, and that was just dandy. Those who still persisted in thinking of themselves as Yugoslavs were now regarded as chumps and hopeless utopians, not even interesting enough to be pitied. In the West many jumped at the opportunity to join in the fun and become ethnic experts. We read countless articles about the rational, democratic, and civilized Croats and Slovenes, the secular Moslems, who, thank God, are not like their fanatic brethren elsewhere, and the primitive, barbaric, and Byzantine Serbs and Montenegrins. This was supposed to explain the breakup and justify the creation of eth-nic states. The concept of the free and unique individual ceased to exist. Someone intermarried and ethnically mixed was an im-pediment to cultural theory. The ideal was a revision of history that a lynch mob could understand.

Anyone who, like me, regularly reads the press of the warring sides in former Yugoslavia has a very different view. The su-preme folly of every nationalism is that it believes itself unique, while in truth it's nothing more than a bad xerox copy of every other nationalism. Unknown to them, their self-delusions and paranoias are identical. The chief characteristic of a true nation-alist is that special kind of blindness. In both Serbia and Croatia, and even in Slovenia, intellectuals are ready to parrot the foulest neofascist imbecilities, believing that they're uttering the loftiest homegrown sentiments. Hypocrites who have never uttered a word of regret for the evil committed by their side shed copious tears for real and imaginary injustices done to their people over the centuries. What is astonishing to me is how many in the West find that practice of selective morality and machismo attractive.

There's no better entertainment than a good bombing, Richard Burt and Richard Pearl, sounding like the disciples of General Mladic, told us a while back on the op-ed page of the *New York Times*. "Air strikes, especially televised ones, would be dramatic, even exhilarating," the two distinguished civil servants claimed. What worries me is the ease with which people even in our democratic society recommend violence to accomplish cer-tain ends, in this case as a bit of uplift and a curative for Amer-ica's lack of military confidence after Vietnam.

In the meantime, columns of refugees. An old woman dressed in black is pulling by a rope a small suitcase that lies flat on the ground. Is she a Moslem from Srebrnica or Zepa, or she is one of two hundred thousand cleansed Serbs from Krajina? It makes no difference. I only catch a glimpse of her on TV, but she moves me as much as that woman suicide we all saw hanging from a tree did. Only a thoroughly evil brain could regard her limping along like that, black as a crow, along the side of a dusty road, and dragging that suitcase as necessary, but the same news program quotes a so-called government expert who sees this "exchange of population as facilitating the peace process." In other words: Innocents everywhere, watch your ass! We got big travel plans for you.

Of course, she reminds me of my mother and me carrying our heavy suitcases in 1948, through pitch-dark Slovenian woods, while sneaking across the border illegally into Austria. The suitcases contained, besides our clothes and a couple of salamis, the yellowed family photographs, the dog-eared diplomas, a few letters, a few other documents covered with rubber stamps, and finally my baby spoon. I wonder what that poor woman is carrying in her suitcase? I'm afraid it would break all our hearts if we found out.

I think this unknown woman's plight is much worse than my mother's and mine ever was. At least we knew that Hitler and Stalin packed our suitcases and Marshal Tito provided the rope. This woman, on the other hand, comes at the end of a long wicked century when everybody is already tired of hearing her rambling story.

In Praise of Invective

... the tongue we use
When we don't want nuance
To get in the way.

—Cornelius Eady

At the end of a murderous century, let's curse the enemies of the individual.

Every modern ideologue and thought policeman continues to say that the private is political, that there is no such thing as an autonomous self, and if there is, for the sake of common good it is not desirable to have one. He or she who refuses to accept the idea that the self is socially constructed and that it can be manipulated to fit the latest theory of human improvement is everywhere the enemy. In the academy of lies where new enthusiasms and hatreds are being concocted, where "only children and madmen speak the truth," as Goebbels said, the unrepentant individual is the one standing in the corner with his face to the wall. Orthodoxy, groupthink, virtue by decree are the ideals of every religion and every utopian model of society. The only intellectual problem that the philosophers of such systems have is how to make conformism attractive. Ideologies from nationism to racism are not really about ideas; they're revivalists' tents offering a chance to the righteous to enjoy their sense of superiority. "We will find eternal happiness and harmony by sacrificing the individual," every congregation of the faithful continues to rhapsodize.

Historical experience has taught me to be wary of any mani-

From *Raritan* 14, no. 3 (winter 1995): 60–64.

festation of collectivism. Even literary historians and critics, when they generalize, make me suspicious. Of course, young poets and painters do associate and influence each other and partake of the same zeitgeist, but despite these obvious truths, what literature worth anything is written by a group? Has any genuine artist ever thought of himself or herself exclusively as a part of a movement? Is anyone seriously a postmodernist, whatever that is?

I don't find systems congenial. My aesthetic says that the poet is true because he or she cannot be labeled. It is the irreducible uniqueness of each life that is worth honoring and defending. If at times one has to fall back on the vocabulary of abuse to keep those in the gumming business away, so be it.

The first and never-to-be-forgotten pleasure that language gave me was the discovery of "bad words." I must've been three or four years old when I overheard my mother and another woman use the word *cunt*. When I repeated it to myself, when I said it aloud for all to hear and admire, I was slapped by my mother and told never to use that word again. Aha, I thought, there are words so delicious they must not be said aloud! I had a great-aunt who used to use such language every time she opened her mouth. My mother would beg her, when she came to visit, not to speak like that in front of the children, but she paid her no mind. To have a temper and a foul mouth like that was a serious liability in a Communist country. "We'll all end up in jail because of her," my mother said.

There are moments in life when true invective is called for, when there comes an absolute necessity, out of a deep sense of justice, to denounce, mock, vituperate, lash out, rail at, in the strongest possible language. "I do not wish to be weaned from this error," Robert Burton wrote long ago in his *Anatomy of Melancholy*. I agree. If anything I want to enlarge and perfect my stock of maledictions.

This is what I learned from twentieth-century history: Only dumb ideas get recycled. The dream of a social reformer is to be the brains of an enlightened, soul-reforming penitentiary. Everyone vain, dull, peevish, and sexually frustrated dreams of legislating his impotence. Mao's uniforms: a billion people dressing the same and shouting from his little red book continues to be the secret hope of new visionaries.

Once one comes to understand that much of what one sees and hears serves to make fraud sound respectable, one is in trouble. For instance, long before Parisian intellectuals did so, my great-aunt had figured out that the Soviet Union and the so-called people's democracies were a scam and a lie from the bottom up. She was one of these women who sees through appearances instantly. To begin with, she did not have a good opinion of humanity. Not because she was a sourpuss, a viper's nest of imaginary resentments. Far from it. She liked eating, drinking, a good laugh, and a quick roll in the hay behind her elderly husband's back. It's just that she had an unusually unclut-tered and clear head. She would tell you that our revolutionary regime, which regarded loose tongues and levity as political crimes and those unfortunates caught in the act as unhealthy elements, was a huge pile of shit, and that included Marshal Tito himself. Her outbursts were caused by what she regarded as other people's gullibility. As far as she was concerned, she was surrounded by cowards and dunces. The daily papers and the radio drove her into verbal fury. "Admit it," she'd yell at my mother and grandmother. "Doesn't it turn your stomach to hear them talk like that?"

If they agreed, and confided in a whisper, that yes, indeed, these Commies are nothing but a bunch of murderous illiterate yokels, Stalinists stooges, and whatnot, she still wasn't happy. There was something about humans as a species that worried her no end. It's not like they were different yesterday and the day before yesterday. This frenzy of vileness and stupidity started on day one. She'd throw her hands up in the air in despair again and again. She couldn't get over it. It was like she had an incur-able allergy to everything false and slimy. It didn't lessen her zest for life, because she had a way of exorcising these evil spirits, but it was a full-time job. Cursing them, I imagine, gave her royal pleasure and, unknown to her, to me, too, listening behind the closed door with a shameless grin.

In a book entitled *Paradoxes of Gender,* Judith Lorber gives us a feminist version of this recurring madness:

> In a world of scrupulous gender equality, equal numbers of girls and boys would be educated and trained for the liberal arts and for the sciences, for clerical and manual labor and for all professions. Among those with equal credentials, women and men would be hired in an alternating fashion for the same types of jobs—or only men would be hired to do women's types of jobs until half of every workplace was made of men and half, women.

Very nice, one thinks, but what about the cops, the jailers, and the informers needed to enforce all of this? Will they be organized in units composed with strict gender equality? We hope so. Note, as is typical of all pious hypocrites and prophets of universal happiness, there's no mention of the individual.

How are we to defend ourselves against these monsters dividing the members of society into useful and useless? For them, the ideal citizen is a voluntary slave! America, or any other place on earth, must be a school of virtue where even the political meaning of a sunset in a poem will be carefully examined for unauthorized views!

I knew a thirteen-year-old who wrote a letter telling off President Johnson about the conduct of the Vietnam War. It was some letter. Our president was an idiot and a murderer who deserved to be napalmed himself, and worse. One evening as the boy and his mother and sister, who told me the story, were sitting around the kitchen table slurping their soup, the doors and the windows leading to the fire escape opened at the same time and men with drawn guns surrounded the table. We are the FBI, they announced, and they wanted to know who was Anthony Palermo? The two women pointed at the boy with thick glasses and crossed eyes. Well, it took a while to convince them that he was the one who wrote the letter. They were expecting a full-grown Commie assassin with long hair and an arsenal of weapons and bombs by his side.

"What do you want from me, blood?" I heard an old woman shout once in a welfare office. She kept cussing them for another five minutes, not because she had any expectation that the wrongs done to her would be righted, but simply in order to make herself feel good and clean for one brief moment.

The Trouble with Poetry

The only thing poetry has always been good for is to make children hate school and jump with joy the day they no longer have to look at another poem. The whole world is in complete agreement on that subject. No one in their right mind ever reads poetry. Even among the literary theorists nowadays, it is fashionable to feel superior to all literature and especially poetry. That some people still continue to write it is an oddity that belongs in some "Believe It or Not" column of the daily newspaper.

When they praised the tribal gods and heroes and glorified their wisdom in war, poets were tolerated, but with the emergence of lyric poetry and the poet's obsession with the self, everything changed. Who wants to hear about lives of nobodies while great empires rise and fall? All that stuff about being in love, smooching, and having to part as the day breaks and the rooster crows is at best laughable. Schoolteachers, clergymen, and other policemen of virtue have always seen eye to eye with the philosophers. No model of ideal society since Plato has ever welcomed lyric poets, and for plenty of good reasons. Lyric poets are always corrupting the young, making them choke in self-pity and indulge in reverie. Dirty sex and disrespect for authority is what they have been whispering into their ears for ages.

"If he writes verses, kick him out," a new father was counseled two thousand years ago in Rome. That hasn't changed a bit. Parents still prefer their children to be taxidermists and tax

From *Michigan Quarterly Review* 36, no. 3 (winter 1997): 39–42, special issue "The Poet's Voice."

collectors rather than poets. Who can blame them? Would you want your only daughter to be a poet or a hostess in a sleazy night club? That's a tough one.

Even true poets have detested poetry. "There are more things beyond this fiddle," said our own Marianne Moore. She had a point. Some of the most idiotic things human beings have ever uttered are to be found in poetry. Poetry, as a rule, has embarrassed both individuals and nations.

Poetry is dead, the enemies of poetry have shouted happily for centuries and still do. Our classic poets, our trendy professors have told us, are nothing but a bunch of propagandists for the ruling classes and male oppression. The ideas once promulgated by the jailers and murderers of poets in the Soviet Union are now a big hit in American universities. Aestheticism, humor, eroticism, and all the other manifestations of the free imagination are suspect and must be censored. Poetry, that foolish diversion for the politically incorrect, has mostly ceased to exist for our educated classes. Nevertheless, as if to spite them, poetry keeps being written.

The world is always looking to reward conformity. Every age has its official line on what is real, what is good and what is bad. A dish made up of dishonesty, ignorance, and cowardice served every evening with a serious mien and an air of highest integrity by the TV news is the ideal. Literature, too, is expected to go along with that. Your tribe is always trying to reform you and teach you manners. The poet is that kid who, standing in the corner with his back turned to his schoolmates, thinks he is in paradise.

If that were not enough, poets, as everybody knows, are champion liars. "You got to lie to stay halfway interested in yourself," says the novelist Barry Hannah. This is especially true of the writers of verse. Every fool one of them believes he perjures himself only to tell the truth. If we can't see the world for what it is in reality, it's due to the layers of dead metaphors poets have left around. Reality is just an old, peeling poetry poster.

Philosophers say that poets delude themselves when they dwell lovingly on particulars. The identification of what remains untouched by change has been the philosopher's task. Poetry and the novel, on the contrary, have been delighted with the ephemeral—the smell of bread, for instance. As far as poets are concerned, only fools are seduced by generalizations.

Heaven and earth, nature and history, gods and devils are all scandalously reconciled in poetry. Analogy says that each is all, all is each. Consequently, the best religious poems are full of the erotic. Subjectivity, so the poets claim, transcends itself by the practice of seeing identity in far-apart things. In a good poem, the poet who wrote the poem vanishes so that the poet-reader may come into existence. The "I" of a total stranger, an ancient Chinese, for instance, speaks to us from the most secret place within ourselves, and we are delighted.

The true poet specializes in a kind of bedroom and kitchen metaphysics. I'm the mystic of the frying pan and my love's pink toes. Like every other art, poetry depends on nuance. There are many ways to touch a guitar string, to kiss and nibble someone's toe. Blues musicians know that a few notes rightly placed touch the soul, and so do lyric poets. The idea is, it is possible to make astonishingly tasty dishes from the simplest ingredients. Was it Charles Olson who said that myth is a bed in which human beings make love to the gods? As long as human beings fall in love and compose love letters, poems, too, will get written.

Most poems are fairly short. It takes longer to sneeze properly than to read a haiku. Still, some of these "little" poems have managed to say more in a few words about the human condition than centuries of other kinds of writing. Short, occasional poems have survived for thousands of years when epics and just about everything else have grown unreadable. The supreme mystery of poetry is the way such poems cast a spell on the reader. The poem is perfectly understandable after one reading, and yet one immediately wants to reread it again. Poetry is about repetition that never gets monotonous. "More!" My sleepy children would nag after I had finished reading them some nursery rhyme. For them, as for all the lovers of poetry, there was only more, and never enough.

It is the paradoxical quality of poetry, precisely, that gives poetry its flavor. Paradox is its secret spice. Without its numerous contradictions and its impertinence, poetry would be as bland as a Sunday sermon or the president's State of the Union address. It's due to its many delicious paradoxes that poetry has continuously defeated and outlived its sternest critics. Any attempt to reform poetry, to make it didactic and moral, or even to restrict it within some literary "school," is to misunderstand its nature. Good poetry has never swerved from its purpose as an inexhaustible source of paradoxes about art and the human condition.

Only a style that is a carnival of styles to bring out poetry's irreverence seems appropriate to me today. A poetry, in short, that has the feel of cable television with more than three hundred channels, facts stranger than fiction, fake miracles and superstitions in supermarket tabloids. A poem that is like a sighting of Elvis Presley on Mars, the woman with three breasts, the picture of a dog who ate Shakespeare's best play, the news that hell is overcrowded, that blackest sinners are now being settled in heaven.

Here, for instance, comes a homeless fellow whose bald head once belonged to Julius Caesar. Didn't I see you holding up a Live Sex Show sign on Times Square yesterday, I ask him? He nods happily. Will Hannibal again cross the Alps with his elephants? is my next question. Watch out for the lady poet, is his reply. If she comes wheeling her shopping cart full of old books and old clothes, be ready to hear a poem.

That reminds me. My great-grandfather, the blacksmith Philip Simic, died at the age of ninety-six in 1938, the year of my birth, after returning home late one night from a dive in the company of gypsies. He thought they would help him fall asleep, but he passed away like that in his own bed with the musicians playing his favorite songs. That explains why my father sang gypsy songs so well and why I write poems, because like my grandfather I can't sleep at night.

Poetry and Experience

Myself, when I'm real

—Charlie Mingus

At least since Emerson and Whitman, there's a cult of experience in American poetry. Our poets, when one comes right down to it, are always saying: *This is what happened to me. This is what I saw and felt.* Truth, they never get tired of reiterating, is not something that already exists in the world, but something that needs to be rediscovered almost daily.

"Nothing is in the intellect which has not been previously in the senses," said Saint Thomas Aquinas, and our poets concur. The Protestant religious tradition of the "inner light" and the British empirical philosophy are the more immediate predecessors of their outlook. The enemy is the abstract philosophical reasoning that strives to describe our human predicament from a priori ideas. The poetry of direct experience distrusts tradition, both in philosophy and in religion, by insisting on the perpetual newness of the world and the sanctity of the individual as the sole repository of the authentic. Each one of us, our poets claim, has the potentiality of being the truth's secretary for a brief spell.

"The soul stays home," Emerson told us. The garden, the kitchen, and the bedroom are as good a place as any to determine our "original relationship to the universe." What I know best is, indeed, always near at hand, and the nearest of them all is my own consciousness. The story of my life is the story of the few extraordinary moments of clarity that have caused me to end up being what I am.

> We wake and find ourselves on a stair; there are stairs below
> us, which we seem to have ascended; there are stairs above
> us, many a one, which go upward and out of sight.
>
> —Emerson

The quality of any experience depends on how aware we are of ourselves while it is taking place. The levels of consciousness can be depicted as a stair of which the lowest step is the sensory and the highest the visionary experience. Where the stairs end, the stairs from the physical to the suprasensuous, the supreme experience of "the timeless in ourselves witnessing time in which it plays no part" begins. We find ourselves briefly in the presence of that *something* that doesn't require our presence, but of which, nevertheless, our presence is a small part. An experience is a remembrance of that moment when we saw everything as if with new eyes. Climbing the stairs we met a stranger who was ourselves. We stood back in astonishment as if before a mirror image.

Lyric poetry at its purest is the phenomenology and metaphysics of that moment and that consciousness. American poetry with its obsessive scrutiny and retelling of experience extends the ambitions of lyric poetry even farther. Everything from Whitman's endless catalogs and Dickinson's miniature inner theaters, to the literary movements such as Imagism with its precise descriptions of inanimate objects, to the so-called Confessional poets with their soul searching and striving to bare their souls to the reader, are a part and a parcel of the same project.

There are at least thirteen ways to complicate this whole issue, as Wallace Stevens knew and demonstrated. What if there's no such thing as pure experience? All experience, Stevens shows in his poems, is interpretation, a synthesis of the given and made up, the conscious and the unconscious.

The one climbing the stair pauses from time to time to close his eyes in revery. Often, it is difficult to say whether what he saw, he saw with eyes open or closed. There are times, too, when we all see far better with our eyes tightly shut.

The unreliability and the ambiguity of sense experience and

the impossibility of language to convey its nuances are not an issue among poets who believe that there can be an unvarnished, direct encounter with reality. For others, like me, analogy with its three alchemical manifestations—simile, metaphor, and symbol—is the true work of poetry.

There is a huge philosophical difference between these two positions, so one forgets that they may occur from the vantage point of the same stair and often even on the same step. One poet sees each thing in its separateness, while another poet detects identities that transcend differences. As the saying goes, it all depends on what you make of your experience.

As I am, so I see.

—Emerson

Sit for fifteen minutes every morning in a hard chair. Collect yourself. Watch yourself doing nothing but watching yourself. Sense the various parts of your body. Divide your attention between the one observing and the one spying on the observer. Note how difficult it is to sustain attention, how the mind wanders, how easily it is distracted, how quickly it forgets its purpose, and so forth. Do this every day for a period of several months and you will understand the differences in the degree of your consciousness and the resulting changes in your psychological state and your thinking and feeling capacity. Eastern thought has always insisted on the necessity of an empirical study of consciousness. Western philosophy has preferred to speculate about its properties as if it were an object outside ourselves and not our most intimate property.

Much philosophical confusion arises from regarding consciousness as a constant, in not realizing that there is a stair, that each step of the stair has a view and a level of intensity peculiar to itself. What is lost sight of again and again is that there are levels of experience, and that each level is determined by the quality of consciousness of that moment.

"Consciousness is the vessel upon whose capacity depends the extent of what is received," the Buddhists say and they are right. If we don't realize that the simultaneous awareness of the knower and the known has fluctuations and nuances and the current reading of our sense perception is not always fully available to us, we are philosophically in trouble.

The kind of consciousness, for instance, that makes an object appear "real," or the kind that makes that object part of our psychic life, or the kind that gives us the impression that we have crossed the Kantian line and are in the presence of "things in themselves," are all worlds apart. Depending on the step one is standing on, one is either a realist or a nature mystic. It comes down to where I remember myself best. There's always one step on the stairs that seems more solid than all the others, the one on which I can put my whole weight and rest for a while.

> There are no words for the deepest experiences.
>
> —Ionesco

The experience of *being* eludes language. We need imagination because the presentness of the present moment cannot be worded except through poetic image. Consciousness is mute. Clarity doesn't need words to tell us our minds are on fire. The words, poets know, can never say what one has seen and felt. The advantage of the poetic image is that it preserves the wordless. It's only through the use of analogy, seeing connections in disparate things, that I can hope to convey the fullness of the original moment. Analogy is a form of translation. I'm seeking an equivalent for the abyss that precedes language.

Poets have a high opinion of figures of speech that is not shared by most other human beings. Only philosophers, who tend to be suspicious of poets, when they don't detest them outright, understand the mad ambition behind the claim. Perhaps only in poetry the bedrock reality and the singularity and the mystery of an individual human life is grasped. Poems witness our existence in ways nothing else can. There's that moment in a great poem when time stops and the reader's self is touched by someone else's life. The poem ascends, and so do we in its company. In a long history of forgetting, poems make us remember what it means to stand naked before ourselves.

Cut the Comedy

> The cow that goes to heaven must take its body for not having enough brain to remember itself in spirit.
> It's an unhappy time of struggle. The cow mooing. It is no less difficult than a breech birth.
> But if a cow should die it must be raised toward heaven, lest it perish in forgetfulness, the sleep of pastures.
> The farmer is trying to get the cow into the hayloft, "nearer, my God, to Thee," pulling the cow with ropes; the cow trying to get a footing over the tractor and bales of hay piled for the ascension . . .
> —The cow mooing, the farmer praying, and his wife crying, scandal, scandal, scandal!
>   —Russell Edson, "The Ascension of the Cow"

If it's funny, then, obviously, it can't be serious, people will tell you.

I disagree. Comedy says as much about the world as does tragedy. In fact, if you seek true seriousness, you must make room for both comic and tragic vision. Still, almost everybody prefers to be pitied than to be laughed at. For every million poems lamenting the cruel fate of a much-misunderstood and endlessly suffering soul, we get one funny Russell Edson or Kenneth Koch poem.

The dirtiest little secret around is that there are as many people without a sense of humor as there are people with no aesthetic sense. How do you convey to someone that something is funny or that something is beautiful? Well, you can't. It's not often that one hears people confess that they don't understand jokes. Humorless folk regard the rest of us as being merely silly.

From *Harvard Review* 11 (spring 1996).

Our verbal acrobatics and our faces distorted by laughter are annoying and childish. Only if they are vastly outnumbered do they plead to have the joke explained. Everyone has, at one time or another, witnessed or participated in such a hopeless attempt. It can't be done. You are better off telling a blind man about the glory of a sunset, and a deaf man about a Charlie Parker solo.

Aesthetic sense can be cultivated or developed, but what of the comic? Is one born with a sense of humor, or can it be acquired?

I suppose both, but it's not easy. If you love yourself too much, your chances are poor. The vainglorious want the world to tiptoe around them and draw near only to gaze at them in wordless admiration. The whole notion of hierarchy and its various supporting institutions depends on the absence of humor. The ridiculousness of authority must not be mentioned. The church, the state, and the academy are in complete accord about that. The emperor who has no clothes always strolls past silent courtiers. All that is spiritual, lofty, and abstract regards the comic as profane and blasphemous.

It is impossible to imagine a Christian or a fascist theory of humor. Like poetry, humor is subversive. The only remedy, the ideologue of all stripes will tell you, is complete prohibition. Moral uplift is a grim business, and the dictatorship of virtue, as we know, has the air of funeral home and graveyard about it. Irony and cutting wit are reserved solely for the superior classes and their closest flunkies. The servants of the mighty and their dogs are allowed to show their teeth and to bite when necessary.

We ordinarily anticipate good literature to be solemn, boring, and therefore edifying. I attended, for example, one of the first performances of Beckett's *Krapp's Last Tape* in New York. The audience in the small theater was made up of intellectual types of both sexes. Early on in the play, the old guy on the stage is trying to open the drawer of the desk he's sitting at. It's stuck. He's got to pull hard and rest between attempts. Finally, it comes loose. He opens the drawer halfway, looks at us, gropes inside and finds what he's looking for. We can't see it, of course, but he can, and he's very happy with his find. Slowly, he brings into view an ordinary banana. After a pause for dramatic effect, he begins to peel it.

At that point, a man sitting behind me began to cackle loudly. To my astonishment people started hissing "Pssst," some even turning around to shake their fists angrily in his face. "Stupid, stupid man," said the beautiful woman sitting next to me. She meant: no side-splitting hilarity allowed in the presence of high art. Like an obedient concertgoer snoozing through a Mahler symphony and awakening at the end to applaud vigorously, we are expected to submit to art and literature as joylessly as to a foul-tasting but beneficial medicine.

Serious literature, supposedly, has an important message to impart, and the problem with the comic is that it does not. In any case, if it has a "message," it's not the one we are comfortable with. The philosophy of laughter reminds us that we live in the midst of contradictions, pulled this way by the head, pulled that way by the heart, and still another way by our sex organs.

Don't forget the eternal shouts of the flesh: Oh! Ah! and Ha-ha!

If humor ever became extinct, human beings would be left without souls.

Philosophically, we must start with the idea of laughter. I cannot imagine anything more horrible than a society where laughter and poetry are prohibited, where the morbid self-absorption of the rich and the powerful and the hypocrisies of our clergymen and politicians go unchecked. Protecting from ridicule those who proclaim eternal truths is where most intellectual energy is expended in our world.

The Greeks, on the other hand, were able to poke fun at their gods.

I ask you, is there anything more healthy than that?

I would consider any society near-perfect where the arts of highest irreverence were practiced and Russell Edson was poet laureate.

Poets' Notebooks

Cheap little dime store notebooks? In the age of the laptop? What is it with these poets, you're probably asking yourselves? How ridiculous can they get? Almost every household in America can choose from a hundred TV channels, and here they are shuffling off to the kitchen, looking for something to sharpen their stub of a pencil with. Do they lick the lead once before they start writing? You can bet on it that some of them do.

Still, the question remains: Why write things down?

The answer is simple: Trusting memory is a bad idea.

My father used to remind us children often that his life's biggest regret was that he never had anything to write with whenever a terrific idea struck him. He expected us to sigh along with him for the great loss to humanity this represented; instead, we just laughed until he got mad and left the dinner table. As it happens, years later his son walks around with pockets containing not one but several writing implements and notebooks.

The habit of note taking is obviously compulsive, like biting one's fingernails. Our culture's need to pigeonhole everything is defeated in notebooks. Spontaneity rules in them. The writer incorporates change and makes do with the unforeseen. The head of a note taker is more like a town dump than a town library.

Oracles are brief and so are poems. The deepest belief of every poem is that less is more. Poems, despite their obscurity, tend to be attempts at clarifications. That aesthetic and philo-

Originally appeared as an introduction in *The Poet's Notebook,* ed. Stephen Kuusisto, Deborah Tall, and David Weiss (New York: Norton, 1995).

sophical premise of poetry makes poets the ideal note takers among us. Reading poetry notebooks, it occurs to me that most literary essays, columns, and even novels would benefit by being cut down to a few sentences.

"So much of what Woolf wrote she wrote not because she was a woman, but because she was Woolf," writes the poet Mary Oliver. Would one want a two-volume study elaborating the idea? Of course not.

"I write in order to make God repent of His sins," says Liz Rosenberg.

A good notebook entry must make us jump. Blasphemy and sex are highly recommended. From the point of groupthink, such manifestations of individuals are nothing but perverse.

"Something totally unexpected, like a barking cat," says Oliver.

"All is transitory," said Buddha, who knew wisdom is not systemizable. Long drawn-out works conflict with the fragmentariness of our consciousness. What is recorded in a notebook is the sense of the unique and unrepeatable experience of those rare moments of clarity. All of a sudden words come to us out of nowhere, true words, words that for some reason we can't find when we want them, when all we get are words that sound hollow. There are insights one either seizes quickly or not at all, like catching flies. It's not by cunning calculation that one captures the flavor of life.

Perhaps we all have a secret belief that lives in their casual detail are more revealing than in the broader outlines. If that were not true, who would care about the private lives of the famous? Individual eccentricities are fascinating. To read our mother's diaries, to peep through the keyhole on the human comedy—that's what we all secretly crave.

I open my notebook and this is what I find:

—"Oh, stay a little longer," Maria Rodriquez telling me one night long ago as we pressed ourselves against the bowling alley wall.

—"Smoocher extraordinaire."

Give your eye glasses a lick.

Live at Club Mozambique.

The map of heaven left on subway.

"A wind sharp enough to peel potatoes" (A. Lundkist.)

Topless Rent-a-Maid.

We all grope around in the dark.

—With his haircut Newt Gingrich makes me think of a lap dog sitting in a rich lady's lap and yelping at the servants.

—Tony says: "Life is like a ladder in a chicken coop: Short and shitty."

Will the computer ever replace the fetishism of the notebook? It's possible, but I doubt it. To hear the poets tell it, the small, handsome notebook and a special pen or pencil are half the work. They are an invitation to write in a certain way. They demand from us absolute conciseness, an aesthetic of modesty. If you write poems on the back of old envelopes and garage sale announcements, as I often do, you don't write epics.

Perhaps you'll even get a notebook of your own and an old-fashioned fountain pen and make your first bold entry in red ink. Just remember, "You got to lie plenty to stay halfway interested in yourself." The novelist Barry Hannah said it, and I can't think of any better advice to give to all the future notebook writers.

The Poetry of Village Idiots

None of the willed imagination of the professionals. No
themes, developments, construction, or method. On the
contrary, only the imagination that comes from the inability
to conform.

—Henri Michaux

I dream of immense cosmologies, sagas and epics reduced to
the dimension of an epigram.

—Italo Calvino

Writing a prose poem is a bit like trying to catch a fly in a dark
room. The fly probably isn't even there, the fly is inside your
head; still, you keep tripping over and bumping into things
while in hot pursuit. The prose poem is a burst of language
following a collision with a large piece of furniture.

So, why do it? What is the attraction of such a seemingly
idiotic undertaking?

In my own case, the so-called prose poems I wrote were the
results of my attempt to get away from myself. To be free of my
own imagination and my own brain, to embark on an adventure
of unforeseeable consequences, continues to be my great dream.

Others pray to God; I pray to chance to show me the way out
of this prison I call myself.

A quick, unpremeditated scribble and the cell door opens at
times. I have never had any idea how I accomplished what I
accomplished. In such writing intuition rules. One depends on
one's own literary savvy to make the right moves and to recog-

From *Verse* 13, no. 1 (1996): 7–8, written for the special issue on prose
poetry.

nize the presence of a poem. For me, the prose poem is a pure literary creation, the monster child of two incompatible strategies, the lyric and the narrative. On one hand, there's the lyric's wish to make the time stop around an image, and on the other hand, one wants to tell a little story.

The aim, as in a poem written in lines, is to arouse in the reader an unconquerable desire to reread what he or she has just read. In other words, it may look like prose, but it acts like a poem. The second, the third, and the fiftieth reading will be even better. You'll never get tired of me, it promises. If you don't believe what I say, read some of Rimbaud's *Illuminations* or Russell Edson's finest poems. They are inexhaustible.

It's pointless to attempt to give guidelines for what is really the product of the free imagination, but I can say the following:

The secret of the prose poem lies in its economy and surprise. It must dazzle, and it must also have a lightness of touch. I regard the comic spirit as its true Muse. Playful and irreverent treatment of every subject is usually the custom. In order to free poetry of its mannerism and ticks, the prose poem must not take itself too seriously. Impossible to write, illegitimate in the view of so many poets and critics, it must remain a pariah and an object of ridicule to survive.

My Insomnia and I

I would not have been the same man if I had been able to sleep well in my life.

It all started when I was twelve. I fell in love. I lay in the dark trying to imagine what was under her black skirt. I thought her name was Maria, but it was really Insomnia.

In a life full of troubles, Insomnia kept me company against the fear of the dark.

We were like young lovers. I had no secrets from her. Our silences were as eloquent as speech.

Most of the time, I resisted the impulse to toss and turn. I didn't blink. I tried not to swallow. I didn't even move my tongue.

My mind was like Ulysses. We took long sea voyages. We were often in South Seas and China. In nineteenth-century London and St. Petersburg we were afraid.

Mostly, though, we were calm. Like Noah's crow we reconnoitered our galaxy. Acrobats of the abyss, face to face with the ineffable.

We had many conversations with old philosophers, mystics, and death camp prisoners:

"I'm awake because I don't wish to be surprised by my future," said one.

"There's freedom only for the awake," said another.

Horror of consciousness, everybody's favorite home movie.

I often felt like a schoolboy condemned to write the same work or two over and over again on the blackboard.

My shoes with their broken and reknotted laces stayed in the corner.

From *Field* 50 (spring 1994): 53–54.

Time vanished. Drunk with its own special brand of melancholy, eternity came to breathe on me.

My fleas didn't sleep well either.

Occasionally, I climbed my own private stairway to the darkest corner of the sky. It was like an empty nightclub with a tragic menu placed on each table.

O soul, nowhere awaited!

The child I was often came to visit me. He wanted to show me things in a theater with mice-eaten red curtains. I went reluctantly, since, of course, he didn't exist. I could've been walking backward on a tightrope with eyes closed.

In the woods one Sunday we came upon a couple lying on the ground. Hand in hand, ourselves fearful of losing our way, we saw what we first surmised was a patch of snow. In a spot rarely visited, we came upon the embraced ones, the two clutching each other naked on the cold ground . . . In the woods that already had a bit of purple shade, some bird chirping and falling silent as we stole by.

At 3 A.M. I always believed the worst. Lying stiffly, counting my heartbeats to a thousand and one!

I pretended to believe in the future, but even so, fits of doubts. Even when I slept soundly, I dreamed I was awake.

My conscience knew its business. I was continuously under its close surveillance. I had a theory: God is afraid of insomniacs, but not the devil.

My love read Victorian novels at night while I read mysteries and history books. The rustle of our pages being turned made the mice in the walls tremble; the angel of death put on his thick glasses to peek over our shoulders.

So many judges, so little justice in the world! Murder is a folk art, it occurred to me in my fiftieth year. They keep perfecting it without ever being pleased with the results.

"Long live the brotherhood of the sleepless!" I shouted with the noose tightening around my neck, but all anyone else heard was the old bedsprings sigh and creak.

And then, just as the day was breaking, I smiled to myself, as I felt my love leaving my side.

Fearful Paradise

We all came to America expecting to play a part in a Hollywood movie. Most of the American films were made in southern California, so if you were in Europe, watching those palm trees swaying in the wind with someone like Rita Hayworth gliding underneath them in a white convertible, you got all kinds of wonderfully wrong ideas about the place. Do people really live like that, I wondered? What will they say about my bad teeth and my funny accent? America was a fearful paradise.

It was reassuring to find that in Chicago, there were poor people. Trash-strewn streets and laundry hanging from fire escapes. Old men swaying on the corner drinking out of brown paper bags. Kids pummeling each other in a school yard. Even a few beggars. This I understood. I immediately felt at home.

Chicago in the fifties was still a town of factories. Its ugliness and squalor brought to mind Dostoyevsky's descriptions of the Moscow and St. Petersburg slums. The people waiting for the North Avenue bus looked as if they had just arrived from Ellis Island. Still, there was plenty of work. An immigrant would come to Chicago, get a job in a factory, and keep it for the rest of his life. He would speak some English, some Polish, some Hungarian, and some Italian because these are the people he worked with. Once, you could say, he knew what he was, to what culture he belonged. Now he was no longer sure.

He worked all the time. The immigrants often had that gray, weary look of people working long hours and weekends, but they had no complaints about that. The neighborhoods smelled

From the *Washington Post,* Sunday, 18 August 1996, C1.

of steaks and fried chicken, where in the old country all you could smell was turnips and cabbage.

The city had an air of prosperity with all the banks, office buildings, and modern apartment houses along the lake, and yet it didn't feel like a big city. After eight o'clock the Loop was dark except for a few movie houses and seedy bars. Hardly anyone was to be found on the streets on weeknights. Perhaps a few farmboys and drunken soldiers loitering outside the Greyhound bus station while the El passed overhead with a face or two pressed to its window, peeking into the dark. In winter it was even worse. There could be a bone-chilling wind blowing off the lake. At least working around the clock kept you warm.

Chicago gave me a better sense of what America was than some small town would have. Its mixture of being, at the same time, very modern and progressive and very provincial is our national specialty. Add to that the realization that so much of our prosperity depends on cheap labor. Immigrants and blacks kept Chicago humming.

I liked the anarchy of the city. There were dives and strip-joints a few blocks away from the monumental Art Institute and the ritzy hotels. Chicago was the garage sale of all the contradictions America could contain. Some rusty water-tower on the top of an old warehouse would look as beautiful as some architectural wonder along the lakeshore. Every notion one had of aesthetics had to be revised if one were to appreciate the city. My greatest teachers, in both art and literature, were the streets I roamed.

Everybody I knew all of a sudden wanted to get educated. If you had to work for a living, as many did, it was night school, of course.

My father was an optimist. He always felt like the money would fall out of the blue sky. He bought the American Dream. It just hadn't been delivered yet. So when I realized soon enough that my parents didn't have the means to put me through school, I attended the University of Chicago at night and worked during the day at the *Chicago Sun-Times*.

Children of immigrants, sons and daughters of blue-collar workers all set out to better themselves. The world of art, literature, philosophy, and sciences opened before us. I wanted to know everything instantly. Anytime I heard a name of a writer or a new idea, I would think: "Oh, God, I'm completely ignorant! I better run to the library and look it up."

The public library was the best place in town. Incredibly, they'd let you take those thick art books home so you could sit in your kitchen, eat your hot dogs and beans, and study the paintings of Giotto and Rembrandt. I took full opportunity of the library's beneficence. I read riding to work: I read while pretending to shuffle papers on my desk; I read in bed and fell asleep with the lights still on.

By the time I arrived for the night classes the next day, I was dead tired. The classes were large, lively. There would always be one or two older students arguing with the teacher, saying things like: "Just because it's written in the book, it doesn't mean it's true." No matter how exhausted everybody happened to be, we all perked up watching the professor squirm.

Older people remembered the Haymarket Riots and other labor unrest. Today everybody behaves as if it was the rich who decided on their own to give their employees the forty-hour week with decent pay. Back then people knew how long it took to make the greedy share a portion of their profits.

Weary or not, I was flying high. I found a small basement apartment on Dearborn, between Goethe and Schiller, in a building now torn down. It had a fancy address, but my place was a rat-infested dump in a crummy old tenement. The Oak Street beach, however, was only a few blocks away. I could go swimming any time I wanted. In local bars, I met budding writers and poets. I even met the famous novelist Nelson Algren at some party.

The second time I bumped into him, I was carrying a volume of Robert Lowell's poetry. "Forget that," he told me. "A kid like you, just off the boat . . . Go read Whitman, read Sandburg and Vachel Lindsey."

I took his advice. I wrote poems like this:

> When I see a cockroach,
> I do not grow violent like the others,
> I stop as if a sign of recognition
> Had passed between us . . .

The literary scene in Chicago was small. One met the same faces, it seems. We'd be squeezed in a room, dark except for a couple of lit candles stuck in Chianti bottles, Charlie Parker and Stan Getz on the cheap, portable record player. The women were dressed in black. Their hair fell down to their shoulders and over their eyes so they gave one the impression they were playing peekaboo all the time. Parisian existentialism had finally come to the Midwest. We were reading Sartre and Camus and quoting them to each other between puffs of cigarette smoke. There'd be a bottle of bad whiskey or rum that tasted like something someone stole from their grandmother's medicine cabinet, but otherwise not much to eat or drink, since everybody was broke.

In the literary crowd, there were many socialists and even a few ex-communists. In those days, much more so than today, radical intellectuals came from working-class backgrounds. They worked with their hands, or they were officials in some union. Jewish, German, Irish fellows who all had plenty of advice for a young poet like me. Beware of the Eastern literary establishment, they told me. You'll end up writing sonnets about Orpheus and Eurydice when you should be writing poems about old ladies who sweep the downtown offices at night.

They had a point. When you're young, and even more so when you're an immigrant, you are looking for role models. You want to blend quickly. I was all ready to put on English tweeds with leather elbow patches and smoke a pipe, but they wouldn't let me: "Remember where you came from, kid," they reminded me again and again.

There's no question they had me figured out. Thanks to them, I failed in my natural impulse to become a phony.

One of the great temptations for an immigrant is to go native the whole way, start eating canned soup, white bread, and Jell-O and hide one's passion for sausages smothered in onions and peppers and crackling in fat. I read Emerson and Thoreau and other New England writers and loved them, but I knew my identity was different. I was already a concoction of Yugoslav, American, Jewish, Irish, and Italian ingredients—and the stew wasn't ready yet. There were more things to add to the pot. More identities. More images to cook.

Here I am on the midnight El riding to work or coming back after a long day. It's winter. It's bitter cold. Every time the door opens, we shiver, our teeth chatter. When it shuts, the heat turned on high and the closely pressed bodies make it even worse. It's hard to keep my eyes open. I'm asleep standing up. If I don't watch it, I'll miss my stop and wake up at the end of the line. I'll be halfway to Iowa. It'll be two o'clock in the morning and I'll be the only one on the open platform pacing back and forth to keep warm, muttering to myself at first, then shouting, shouting at the top of my lungs:

"What a life! What a city! What a country!" And I'm leaving out the cuss words.

My Unwritten Books

In a room with a noisy window-fan I'm reading Meister Eckhart's sermons, the one in which he says: "The moment in which God made the first man and the moment in which the last man will disappear, and the moment in which I'm speaking are all one and the same moment."

Little ideas and big ideas are buzzing in my head when I look up from the book and see my grim face looking back at me from the mirror across the room.

Thoreau loved ants. He'd meet one in the morning and spend the whole day talking to him. Poe often dreamed he was a black pullet pecking in the graveyard on moonlit nights. Hawthorne kept a rusty nail in his shoe as a pet. Melville nursed his melancholy by eating fresh strawberries in cream on summer mornings. Come evening, Emily Dickinson could see the shadow her brain cast on the bedroom wall. Whitman's beard once caught fire. The firemen came from as far as Louisiana to put it out. Emerson said, "The world is an immense picture book." "Everybody's using its pages to wipe his ass," wrote in response an unknown American genius in the margin of my library book.

The air is full of flying cinders this morning. Whole neighborhoods could be going up in flames while the children chase each other in the playground, while they kick the one fallen against the high, peeling wall of the school they go to and scream in mock terror, fleeing the girl with crossed eyes. All

---

From the *Ohio Review* (forthcoming).

that, mind you, behind a rusty fence firmly secured with a chain and a heavy padlock.

The windows of Hotel du Nord have a view of the snows of Labrador that are famous for their yellow sunflowers. The white paint in our room is peeling; the old beds and chairs have gone to China to be missionaries; the desk clerk is as deaf as a shoe brush. When somebody knocked, we ran to open. There was never anyone there. The quiet that reigns in the hotel is like that of an Egyptian pyramid in a hundred-year-old postcard with an address in Oklahoma on the other side.

The sky is blue and so is the ceiling. Glued to the wall, there's a cutout of a blonde child pointing to a picture of a camel that could have come out of a long-discontinued breakfast cereal. Over him, hung from a silver rod by a metal hook, there's a postage stamp with a picture of another smaller child dressed in a Renaissance costume. This one appears to be saying his bedtime prayer. Their father, the prince, has gone off to stand on the parapet with his beard and hair dripping red paint.

If the night ever falls, we will light matches and invite the children to be our guests at a meal of watch wheels and watch faces.

The kid torturing the cat next door has a great future in store for him. His mama loves him, his daddy does too. They live in a pretty white house with two columns. Their trimmed hedges and trees keep their sober dignity even when I yell for him to stop.

He sits on his back steps lonely, sweet-looking and idle. The cat is nowhere to be seen. The weather is beautiful.

Angelic birdseed on the tip of Martha's pink tongue while she speaks of her faith in God's benevolence.

It was the first day of spring. Birds were singing. Romeo loved the smell of his shit, but when he smelled Juliet's rose-scented farts, he ran out on the balcony screaming, give me air.

Old man eating soup with his hat on, slurping and wiping his mouth with a sleeve while pointing with the spoon at the crows sitting on the top of a white church. Like the devil himself, he says. Yes sir, like the devil himself.

In a zoo I noticed many animals who had a fleeting resemblance to me.

"Dear Comrade Stalin," he wrote, "my dream is to see the whole world become a collective poultry farm."

At Nick's, today's special was bean soup with sausage. You could hear everybody ordering it, even the bag lady we often saw sleeping in doorways.

"I used to read palms for a living," she told me with her mouth full. And then, taking a swig from a brown paper bag from under the table, "Lift your hand, everybody, so that I may read your future."

The evening is coming. Someone milks a black cow. Someone reloads a different gun at the fair and fires. *Return of the Invisible Man* is on the late show, someone says as he bends down to pick a wild poppy in the darkening meadow.

As the curtain goes up, there's a gasp of surprise and terror from the audience. The lovers on the stage have two heads on the same shoulder. They're sitting in the same chair at the same round table gazing at each other lovingly.

People rarely doubt what they see, more often they doubt what they think, says one head to the other. We in the audience are too busy counting the lovers' eyes and noses to listen to their words.

The twelve girls in the gospel chorus sang as if dogs were biting their asses.

A dream: In a burning house I'm reading a book on fire.

The July night was smothering the avenue with its steamy kisses. The purse-snatchers were already cracking their knuckles in doorways while we strolled arm in arm, stopping only to grab each other by the crotch and talk breathlessly of Calabrian sausages and Romano cheese.

The entire play consists of monologues and asides by a dozen actors who are on the stage all at the same time. They pay no attention to each other even though their speeches are inordinately passionate. They rant, snort, foam at the mouth for almost three hours. One of the actresses is stark naked, one of the actors is dressed as a general, another has a rope around his neck, there's an old woman scrubbing the floor under his feet and a dog who walks on his hind legs.

And in the background, canned laughter by a Chinese audience.

Melancholy Senorita Miranda waiting for me on her veranda. "I'm an obituary writer on a holiday," I said to her.

"When the entire world was covered with ladybugs," she sighed, "and we made love on the ceiling."

Dog races in dreams: I occasionally saw a man on all fours trying to keep up.

Compose yourself, my friend, these must be the madonnas of Hieronymus Bosch riding the A-train after midnight.

"Do I look like Nostradamus?" he says to his reflection in the window of a store selling fire-damaged furniture.

I ask about heaven and hell. X ponders with eyes closed. Y continues to gorge himself on bread and butter, and Z studies the ceiling as if it were his navel.

The plot thickens. Nadine barges in wearing a new black bikini. She wants to know what we think of it? We think she ought to turn around, once, twice . . . except for Z, who continues to regard the ceiling with a beseeching air.

Early one morning a young woman in black dress and high heels fishing from a bridge on the way to Portsmouth.

I only have my king left on the chessboard, and he is cornered, while my invisible opponent has all his figures still in play.

"It must be one of the World's Great Masters I'm playing?" I shout.

"It's your fate, dummy," the naked woman in bed says.

"In that case," I tell her, "come over and sit in my lap. After we get nice and snug, I'll think of some clever move."

I shared the solitude of my childhood with a black cat. I sat on the window for hours on end watching the empty street while she sat on the bed washing herself. When night fell, I lay on the bed and she watched the street.

Round about midnight, the phone in the booth on the corner would ring a long time, but no one ever came to answer it. After that the cat's tail would flicker a long time until it put me to sleep.

On rainy days, I played chess with the cat, who pretended to doze. Once, when my mother turned on the table lamp, the silhouettes of the few remaining chess figures could be seen clearly on the wall. I was afraid to move. I didn't even take a breath.

When I finally did, the cat had vanished, taking the chess set with it and leaving me as I was in the same mean little room with its one window and its view of the empty street.

Child of the night, hold a mirror in your hand like an open book and call out the names of your father and mother, first name, last name, as they were called out long ago on their first day of school. When your neighbor bangs on the wall, shout even louder, shriek! while watching them stare back at you out of the dim mirror.

A cold, clear night, good for radio reception of distant stations, some peddler of the divine from across the continent.

I remember soaping the crotch of a certain Miss L. in the sea at dusk, while she soaped mine. The water was cold, but we were burning. Our kisses made the sun take its time setting.

Eye to eye with the fly on the wall. "My luck quit for a while," he says. "I see yours is holding still."

I ran into the poet Mark Strand on the street. He immediately challenged me by drinking a glass of red wine while standing on his head. I was astonished! He didn't even spill a drop. It was the same bottle that the great French poet, Charles Baudelaire, never got to finish because his mistress crawled into the room on all fours looking for one of her hairpins.

"Is this what is called magic realism?" I asked him. Years ago this same Strand translated a Quechua poem about a man raising a fly with wings of gold in a green bottle, and now look at him!

In B. everyone's first name seems to be Homer. The local pastime is slapping mosquitos on each other's foreheads. The blind photographer sits on the porch snapping pictures of his barking dog. The mortician's young wife sings like a bird in a cage when she hangs her laundry.

"I suffer from a rare variety of bad luck which has an occasional unexpected happiness in store for me," the beggar said to me.

My bad luck, on the other hand, loves to entertain me with its practical jokes. I had just learned how to say, "More cookies Mom," when a German bomb fell on the house across the street. No sooner had I learned how to ride a bike than luck decorated the trees along country roads with men hanging from its branches. And so it went.

You're fifty-eight years old today. It's Sunday, so school is out except for a couple necking in the front of the classroom. Their tongues, which go around each other, are savage with ink.

You close your eyes to make sure. You open them again to

verify the wiped blackboard, the wall clock for some reason cadaverous to read, while the two of them exit, the girl on crutches, dragging her foot behind.

It's raining and the sidewalks are slippery. He walks quickly with a schoolbook over his head, the one on crutches, falling behind with each step, shouts to him to not to worry, to hurry home . . .

A hearse with a coffin stopped by the movie house so that its driver could shoot the breeze with the ticket seller. The movie showing was called *Diabolique*.

A complete stranger came to me one night on Forty-fourth Street and said I reminded him of his dead brother.

Every night I go down on my knees just to say this in your keyhole:

"Peddler of falsehoods, lover of death's latest gadgetry, murder's helper, instigator of lynching mobs, gourmet of other people's sufferings," etc., etc.

"Hey, fart catcher," he shouts from the inside! "Small-beer philosopher, king of bird shit working yourself into a fit, your kind was born only to be stepped on like roaches," etc., etc.

The infinite riches of an empty room. Silence makes visible what now appears to be the most interesting grain of dust in the whole world.

Miniature philosophers: the kind you keep in your pocket. Are you Pico della Mirandola? I said to the tip of a toothpick lying in the palm of my hand. If so, make me think big thoughts on subjects the world regards as being of no consequence.

It's so quiet, I can hear that something which is always eavesdropping on my life make a slight noise, the kind a letter makes sliding into a mailbox that has no name.

Better knock on wood, I thought, making the stopped clock on the dining-room table jump with the three loud knocks.

My philosophical views were shrouded in obscurity. My only true disciple was a black cat who kept crossing the street in front of me, making me stop dead in my tracks.

Everyday a nervous fit. Why do you keep staring at me like a professor of algebra? I asked my conscience. Go back to your seat, dummy, he ordered me, while I kept mulling over new ways to insult him.

Why is that we never laugh when we tickle ourselves? I shouted from the last row. How come some girl only has to wag her little finger at us and we plop down cackling on the floor, begging her for mercy?

Think about it, too, I said to the puss coming over to rub herself against my leg on the street.

Time Channel

We have a television channel that forecasts hours and minutes. The host wears black, like an undertaker, and points at a huge clock with a stick. We watch the future change into the past before our eyes. How boring, you must think. I admit there is a certain monotony, a certain lulling indolence. Some people watch this channel because at least there won't be any surprises. Others, like myself, dream of the impossible: the demon of change with his finger in the gears of the clock, minutes, hours mislaid.

The host explains that if we pay close attention, we'll see the long hand of the clock move. It's true. It twitches. You might even say it has a nervous tick. The short hand, however, appears stuck, and that's why I watch. In exactly sixty minutes, the host predicts, the short hand will have moved to the next number. My eyes don't leave the clock. I blink and blink and see nothing. The short hand has now reached two, and the host confirms the fact in a voice tinged with triumph.

There is also a thin, quick-moving hand that indicates seconds. It moves so quickly that, by the time you ask yourself where it is, it is somewhere else. Time is everywhere and yet nowhere. Every now is already a then.

The evening host wears a striped suit, an Elvis Presley wig, and a big smile. He claps his hands, announcing happily: "Here comes eleven o'clock." He scratches his head and says: "If nothing were to pass away, there would be no time." Or, just before a commercial: "In Paris, the night is already over, while in San Francisco, dusk is just falling."

From *Grand Street* 54 (fall 1995): 34–35.

The commercials peddle the usual stuff: potato chips, Caribbean cruises, used cars at incredibly low prices. The more uncommon items are a board game called Zeno's Paradox and a California wine—one sip of which can supposedly change the direction of time.

At midnight a dark-haired lady comes to serve as a host. Her name is Lana Malone. She wears a tight red dress to accentuate her hourglass figure. She speaks in hoarse whispers as if confiding a great secret. It's ten to four, she'll say, and your heart skips a beat. My friend Freddie, who is an even greater insomniac than I am, and who stays up all night checking the accuracy of his watch, heard her say one night between official announcements: "When you kiss me, sweetheart, the world stops turning."

Time exists only where counting exists and counting is an activity of a lonely soul. So, turn on your television set and flick past the channel of the gypsy fortune-tellers, past the channel devoted to insane asylum inmates, past the channel that shows reruns of old state executions, to the channel that tells the time.

Dinner at Uncle Boris's

Always plenty of good food and wine. The four of us at the table take turns uncorking new bottles. We drink out of water glasses the way they do in the old country. "More bread!" somebody yells. There's never enough bread, never enough olives, never enough soup. We are eating through our second helping of thick bean soup after having already polished off a dozen smoked sausages and a couple of loaves of bread.

And we argue with mouths full. My uncle Boris would make Mother Teresa reach for a baseball bat. He likes to make big pronouncements, to make the earth tremble with his political and artistic judgments. You drop your spoon. You can't believe your ears. Suddenly, you are short of breath and choking as if you swallowed a big fly.

"Is he kidding?" I hear myself say, my voice rising to a falsetto.

I am the reasonable type. I try to lay out the pros and cons as if I were a judge making a summation to the jury. I believe in the calming effect of an impeccable logical argument. Before I can get very far, my brother interrupts to tell that I'm full of shit. His philosophy is: the more reasonable it sounds, the less likely it is that it's true. My father, on the other hand, always takes the Olympian view. "None of you know what the fuck you're talking about," he informs us and resumes slurping his soup.

Before we can all gang up on him, the pork roast is served. The skin is brown and crusty with a bit of fat underneath. There are potatoes and onions in the pan, soaked in the drippings. We are in heaven. The new bottle of wine is even better. Nuit Saint

From *Creative Nonfiction*, no. 7 (1996): 89–93.

Georges is my father's favorite wine, since his name is George. That's the only one he buys when he is flush.

For a while we don't say anything. We just grunt with our faces in our plates. My aunt is carving more meat while my uncle runs into the kitchen to get those hot little red Mexican peppers he forgot all about.

Unfortunately, one of us starts on politics. Immediately, we are arguing again. In the last few years Boris has become very conservative. He loves Barry Goldwater. He loves Nixon. As for Bobby Kennedy, he's a Russian agent, if you ask him. Boris even warned the *New York Times* about that, but they didn't print the letter, of course. Tonight he shouts that I am a communist too. He has suspected it for years and had his final proof just two minutes ago.

I have no idea what I said to make him think that, so I ask him to please repeat it. He's appalled. No guts, he says. Feigning innocence, backtracking. Jesus Christ! He calls on the heavens to witness.

"It's what you said about Hoover," my brother says, guffawing. Both he and my father are enjoying themselves while I'm debating where to punch Boris in the mouth. He's really pissed, too. He says I even look like Trotsky with my wire-rimmed glasses. "Get me the FBI on the phone," he yells to my aunt. He's going to speak to J. Edgar personally about me.

It's hard to tell with Boris if he's entirely serious. He loves scenes. He loves opera. It's the third act, we are all dead on the stage, and he is caterwauling. Without histrionics life is boring. This is bliss, as far as he's concerned.

Watching him rant like that, I get an inspiration. I rise from the table, walk over, and solemnly kiss him on the top of his bald head. He's stunned speechless! It takes him some time to collect himself. Finally, he smiles sheepishly and embraces me in turn.

"Forget about the FBI," he yells to my aunt in the kitchen.

She comes out with enough different cheeses to open a store. We eat and drink and converse politely. The old guys are reminiscing about the war.

Is it true one grows nostalgic even about the horrors as one grows old? Probably. I'm nostalgic about an August afternoon after the war. My mother, brother, and I were being escorted at gunpoint and on foot from one prison to the other. At some point we walked past an apple orchard, and our guard let us stop and pick apples. Not a care in the world. Munching the apples and chatting with our guard.

As for my father and Boris, it seems that when they were in Trieste they used to pull this stunt. My father would invite friends to a fancy restaurant, but when time came to pay the bill, he'd send Boris to break the news that they were completely broke to the unsuspecting owner.

"You were very good at it," my fathers assures him.

Boris, when he's not raving, looks like an English gentlemen and has the appropriate clothes and fine manner to go along with his face. The owner of the restaurant would accept his apologies and his promise to settle the bill expeditiously, and would even permit his financially strapped guests to order another round of brandies before going off into the night.

"It's his smile," we all agree. Boris has the sweetest, shiest smile when he's happy. Old ladies, especially, adore him. Nobody knows how to bow and kiss their hands like he does. It's hard to believe he was once a guard in a maximum-security penitentiary in Australia. Come to think of it, none of us, individually or collectively, make much sense. We are all composite characters, made up of a half dozen different people, thanks to being kicked around from country to country.

Boris, for instance, right now is singing. He studied opera singing for years, tried to make a career of it, and failed. Now he sings only when he's happy. He has a huge, beautiful tenor voice, but no ear. When he starts hitting the high notes, you have to run for your life. It's no use. He can be heard across the street. He has the world's loudest voice and it's off key.

He sings for us an aria from *Otello*. We survive that somehow, but he's not through yet. We are going to hear Tristan's death scene. Across the table my father looks grim. My brother has vanished. I am lying on the floor at Tristan's feet trying my best to keep a straight face. Boris paces up and down conducting the Berlin Philharmonic as he sings. From time to time he stops to translate for us. "Tristan is going mad," he whispers. No doubt about that! This Tristan is ready for the loony bin. His tongue is lolling and his eyes are popping out of his head. He's standing on the sofa and leaning against the wall, arms spread, as if he is about to be crucified.

"Verflucht wer dich gebrant!" he shrieks.

"Stop it, Boris," my aunt says calmly, coming in from the kitchen with the cake.

"Please let him sing the death scene, auntie," I say, and now even my father has to grin.

You have to admire the man's love of music. Boris confessed to me once that he could never sing in the real opera house. He'd get so excited on the stage, he'd jump into the orchestra pit at the conclusion of his aria.

Now we applaud him. We are thirsty and hungry again and so is he, luckily. My brother has reappeared.

"I'm going to bed," my aunt announces after she brings back the cheese and cold cuts. She knows this is not going to end soon. We are on our favorite topic, the incredible stupidity of our family.

I don't know if all large families indulge in such orgies of self-abuse, but we made a speciality of it. I don't think it's pretense either. I mean, it's not like we believe secretly we are really superior and this is just talk. Our family history is a story of endless errors of judgment, of bad situations made even worse by bickering.

"Imagine this," my father says. "There's a war on, the Nazis, the Ustashi, the Hungarians, the Romanians, the Chetniks, the Italians, the Bulgarians, the Communists are killing us, and even the English and the Americans are dropping bombs. So, what do we do to make things really interesting? We all take different sides in that war so we can really make life miserable for each other."

We are silent with the weight of our drunkenness and the sad truth of my father's last remark. Finally, Boris looks up and says: "How about a really great bottle of wine?"

We all look at Boris puzzled, but he explains that this wine is supposed to be very special, very old, very expensive.

"What is it?" we want to know.

He's not telling. He's going to decant it in the cellar so we can blind-taste it and guess its origins.

Very well. Off he goes, and he's gone so long we are beginning to think the bastard sneaked off to bed. Instead, he returns with an air of mystery carrying a bottle wrapped in a towel. The last time Boris had a bottle of expensive wine he had us sip it from a teaspoon. He went around the dinner table pouring drops of a fine old Margot into a spoon and making us all in turn say "aaaaaahh" like a baby doctor.

This time we just get clean glasses and he pours everybody a little taste. It's red wine. There's no doubt about that even at three in the morning. We twirl it in our glasses, sniff it like real pros and take a sip. I think it's Chianti, my father says it's a Burgundy, my brother mentions Spanish wine, but is not sure.

Boris is triumphant! Here's the final proof! Serbs as a people, and the members of this family especially, are all know-nothings, show-offs, and the world's biggest phonies.

Then, to rub it in, he tells us how he found out recently that the Sicilian who pumps his gas in Brooklyn makes his own wine. "Probably in the same bathtub where he washes his ass," he adds for effect. Anyway, the man gave him a bottle for Christmas and this is what we are drinking.

It still tastes pretty good, but on second thought, we have to admit, we made complete fools of ourselves. Of course, we can barely keep our eyes open. The day is breaking. For the moment we have run out of talk. We just look at each other, yawning occasionally. The house is quiet. The city is quiet. Even the cops are catching forty winks in their patrol car on the corner.

"How about some ice cream?" Boris asks.

On Dreams

Rest during the day so you can sleep well at night.
—Ancestral wisdom

There were periods in my life when I couldn't remember a single dream. I went around embarrassed, trying to imagine what dreaming would be like. At other times I found myself every night with a different cast of characters dressed like guests at a funeral. More freaks packed in one dream than in all the sideshows in the world. I acted in many tragedies and porn flicks. The sets and the lighting were that of a 1920s German expressionist movie. There was a lot of shadow where further dangers lurked. The sky in my dreams was always overcast. I was in some vaguely familiar city where, for some reason, I could not give my terrors a slip. Everyone must have walked on padded feet, because there was never any sound.

> I dreamed of a school of insomnia where I studied hard in the back seat of an empty classroom.

> I dreamed of a lollipop in the shape of a skull.

> I dreamed of my father on his knees nibbling wildflowers.

> Once I permitted myself to be fired from a cannon.

> Everyone I met looked younger, even the dead.

> I dreamed of a woman picking my pocket in the street, and that woman was Veronica Lake.

From *Harvard Review,* no. 7 (fall 1994): 13–14.

I dreamed of the silence of the Sahara Desert.

Have researches ever been made into the wretched loneliness of the dreamer?

The beast loves to be lied to.

On the night of February 7, 1959, I dreamed I was Stalin's secretary. I walked around with adoring countenance, terribly afraid and at the same time ashamed of myself.

I dreamed of a monkey with a rosary.

I dreamed I barked back at a dog.

Fairy-tale stuff . . . like eating soup with a pin.

It was like watching myself through dark glasses on a rainy evening.

I dreamed I was naked with M. on the crowded subway and she wanted me to make love to her.

I found myself inexplicably in the same seaside hotel again and again embracing the hips and moist sex of a woman whose face I could not see.

A Chinese monastery in the mist—what the hell was I doing there?

Were these scenes of the future life or the consequences of eating a large pepperoni pizza at bedtime?

Truth is either what can be communicated, or what has no hope of ever being communicated.

Dreams, you're as dumb and as unintelligible as history!

My happiness was just around the corner and so was my death.

I fell off buildings repeatedly. I tried to flap my arms in a hurry or hold myself back by grabbing my head by the ears, but it was no use.

And I've never ever seen the moon in dreams!

Jane Kenyon

The kind of short lyric poem Jane Kenyon was a master of is one of the great wonders of the world. Epics grow unreadable, empires collapse, languages and cultures die, but short lyric poems written two thousand years ago still engage us. Ezra Pound used to claim that "all ages are contemporaneous." What the lyric poem says is that all present moments since the beginning of the world are. That's what makes an old Egyptian or Chinese poem still understandable and still moving. We all know what it's like to live the moment.

How strange I should be alive in this very moment. How strange the knowledge that I shall die one day. These facts are faced again and again in poems. The awe, the terrifying realization that this should be so is not easy to put into words. The drama of being unable to say what we feel most deeply is the subject of lyric poems. At the heart of the lyric, as Jane Kenyon knew very well, language fails us. The experience of the naked moment is incommunicable except in the finest lyric poems.

At the point where time, eternity, history, and consciousness meet, the little poem leaves a trace of an individual's life. The sounds, the colors, the smells, the tastes, the flashes of insight all crowd into that single moment. In the small space of the poem, loves, fears, and passions find ample room. The short lyric poem of ten to twenty lines is long enough to include both heaven and earth.

As it does so, it rejects preamble and argument. The lyric poem's proof is in its voice. Somehow the poet makes us trust her voice. I say "somehow" because it's hard to be precise about

From *Columbia Review,* no. 26 (1996): 172–73.

the strategy in any poem that gives us a sense of hearing a living voice. All that comes from deepest emotions and most intense visions and radiates from the core of a good poem eludes critical analysis.

I only have hunches. Reading Kenyon's poems, I have a feeling that every one of her words was placed on the page in the full consciousness of its intellectual and emotional weight. Poetry, she reminds me, is the work of weighing words on a scale finer than the one pearl merchants and diamond cutters use. This work, of course, can only be done in solitude and in silence. That's the voice of the poems. A voice shadowed by solitude and silence.

It's like coming upon someone we know and love lost in reverie. When we touch them and ask them what they're thinking of, they're unable to tell us. We assume they can, but won't, but this is not the case. Jane's poems measure the gap between language and what it presumes to name. That distance to her at times appears infinite, and that is the cause of her melancholy. She is the poet who opens her being toward everything that is unnameable and unknowable. Lyric poetry for her, to paraphrase Chekhov, is that illness for which many remedies are prescribed and for which there's no cure.

The Greeks suspected that the gods are jealous of lyric poets. The human heart can generate mysteries even they, immortals, are not capable of equaling. The gods can do everything and understand everything except what it's like to be mortal. Here I'm tempted to propose what I feel to be the paradox of Jane Kenyon's poetry and the source of her power as a poet. She is a deeply religious woman who speaks to the Lord, not of the immortal soul, but of the beauty of what passes away and is bound to be forgotten. Only in the very finest poems, the kind she wrote, do we have lasting record of our naked humanity.

Ingeborg Bachmann

I am a dead man who wanders registered nowhere

I first read Ingeborg Bachmann some thirty years ago in Jerome Rothenberg's small anthology of young German poets. I liked her poems immediately, even though Hans Magnus Enzensberger, Paul Celan, and Günter Grass with their radical imagery suited my taste for novelty much more. In fact, there is nothing obviously modern about Bachmann's poems if one thinks of modernism as a tradition that includes expressionism, dada, and surrealism. Such poems tend to be programmatically irreverent and antipoetic. In contrast, Bachmann wrote in a manner that would not have seemed entirely unfamiliar to the great Romantic poets, that is, until they started reading her closely and realized her profound difference.

I myself remember being made uneasy even at my first encounter. Here was a poetry of sublime lyricism that suggested the knowledge of the horrors of World War II without employing any of its familiar images. Bachmann had a way of writing about nature such that it reminded one of concentration camps, as it were. In every new anthology of German poetry that subsequently came out, I sought her out, and when I found the same few poems that kept being translated over and over again, I experienced once more her spell. Very simply, I knew that I had just read a poet that I would never forget.

This is one of the true mysteries of literature. What is it that makes certain poems immediately memorable? Obviously, it

From foreword to *The Collected Poems of Ingeborg Bachmann* (New York: Marsilio Publishers, 1994), xi–xiv.

could be the sheer mastery of form and the originality of the imagination that captivate us. Still, this is not always an explanation. Tastes change, newness wears out. Poems that once seemed unforgettable because of their shocking imagery or content suddenly cease to seduce us. Long after the dazzling virtuosity of one kind or another, the absence of something far more important becomes noticeable. I have here in mind that elusive property known as the poet's voice. In the case of Bachmann, it is not so much what she says, or even how she says it; rather it is her voice that one always remembers. A voice that touches the heart. One could go so far as to claim that the sound of a living voice is all that lyric poetry conveys.

The voice is the imprint of individuality. The tone of one's voice, as everybody knows, varies depending on the attitude one takes toward the words one is saying. In poetry, it is the voice that brings the breath of the living human being to us. The tone either persuades us that what is being said matters, or it does not, and that tone cannot be contrived. Here's someone bearing witness to her consciousness and the wonder of its existence. The world is a strange place, and what is even more strange is that I should be alive in it today! No grammar of that sensation is possible, as Emily Dickinson knew. She also understood that poets aim to recreate in their poems the feel of that *something* which cannot be put into words.

The preoccupation of so much post-1945 poetry in Germany and elsewhere is language. Are there any words still left around that one can trust? It is the weight of the unsavable that gives Bachmann's poetry its tragic dimension.

> Where Germany's earth blackens the sky,
> a cloud seeks words and fills the crater with silence.

She takes into account the profound philosophical and moral difficulty of being a poet in an epoch of history's greatest murderers, an epoch furthermore in which whatever explanations of evil we once turned to for solace have become inadequate. The death of God, you may say, is no big deal if everybody behaves well, but once the slaughter of the innocent starts, how do you catch any sleep at night? An air of permanent crisis and terror, surrounding all human endeavor, is our inheritance.

> War is no longer declared,
> but rather continued. The outrageous
> has become the everyday. The hero
> is absent from the battle. The weak
> are moved into the firing zone.
> The uniform of the day is patience,
> the order of merit is the wretched star
> of hope over the heart.

If that was all there was to it, our predicament would be far more clear. But, there is another paradox. Yes, unimaginable crimes and sufferings have occurred, and yes, the world is still beautiful. There are still trees, lovers, and children, and they go about their business as if nothing had happened. After all the nightmares and gloomy thoughts one has had, it is astonishing to find innocence. Is it possible to be happy in a world that has seen such horrors, Bachmann continuously asks herself? Does that knowledge always doom one to despair and the inability to relish life for what it is?

> I am the child of great fear for the world,
> who within peace and joy hangs suspended
> like the stroke of a bell in the day's passing
> and like the scythe in the rope pasture.
>
> I am the Continual-Thought-of-Dying.

Bachmann's is a poetry of estrangement and nostalgia. Her poems are elegies for a loss beyond words. She is the one made stranger in the midst of her own people by that knowledge, the one condemned to remain forever standing on the threshold. "Our Godhead, history, has ordered for us a grave from which there's no resurrection," she says. Her poems have an awareness of the tragic worthy of the Greeks. She is the poet of the long, dark night of history and the lone human being awake in it. It is her heroic refusal to make things intellectually and morally easy for herself that gives her poems heroic stature and nobility.

In a century of displaced persons, Bachmann's poetry, appropriately, is full of voyages and partings. This prodigal daughter knows that we cannot ever say what our fates truly mean; we can only try to convey endlessly how things appear to us. Every day we say farewell to some small epiphany that made the world so vivid and meaningful yesterday. Whoever in the future wishes to experience that all-pervading sense of exile our age has felt should read Bachmann, just as we must be immensely grateful that Peter Filkins has now given us the fullest and the best translation we have in English of this magnificent poet.

Don Quixote Charging a Pineapple

The old tradition of books illustrating the wonders of the far reaches of the earth still lives on in the art of Saul Steinberg. I have in mind those so-called true accounts of travelers and explorers who write about the fabulous cities and animals they have come across on their journeys. We hear of ants who dig for gold, men who have hands where their ears should be, men born without mouths who feed on smells, trees capable of human speech, orchards that bear scissors and toy windmills, birds who carry a horse and a rider to their nest, cities that like dreams are made of our secret wishes, and much else that no one has ever met with even in their wildest imagining.

America, for Steinberg, is such a place. He saw a man carrying his exact double over his shoulder. He saw a bust of a woman sitting on a TV table that had wheels. On her head were rabbit ears, while from her back a long cord extended that could be plugged into an electric outlet. He saw a cat with a sword riding a peacock. He saw Uncle Sam playing the violin and Lady Liberty playing a toy drum on a street corner for a couple of dancing ants. He saw a man removing his nose as if it were a pair of wire-rimmed glasses. He saw a mob of question marks facing soldiers with their guns pointed. He saw art museum visitors carefully examining half a dozen blank canvases. He saw the Dove of Peace flying with a knife in its beak. He saw a fat baby with a hammer about to smash the globe of the world.

It is a complex fate to be an American.

—Henry James

I once stopped in a pink motel on the Kansas prairie for the night. A single pickup truck with an empty gunrack was parked outside one of its rooms, and that was all there was except for a huge satellite dish blocking the sunset. Miles and miles of flat country in all directions. No gas pump, fast-food stand, or any other human dwelling in sight. Not even a distant silo.

Tired from the long drive, I immediately started undressing to take a shower, turning the TV on to keep me company, but I never got to the bathroom. The room may have been small and ratty, but the TV had over three hundred channels. I stood half-naked flicking the channels with the remote control in growing astonishment and disbelief. Images flashed by quickly. Too many images.

"Hell has burst forth and has poured forth its abundance," some preacher would have shouted. Indeed, there were plenty of preachers on the screen to pick from. Here was America in all its bewildering variety and terror Steinberg knew so well. I could switch from a church service to a view of a couple ripping each other's clothes off before hopping into bed, a slow golf game, a World War II documentary with bombs still falling on some burning German city, a political advertisement for a congressman promising family values and lower taxes, a little blind girl playing the accordion on a Canadian amateur hour, a faith healer screaming at an old woman to throw down her crutches, the Playboy talk show with all its participants in the nude discussing modern-art collecting, the dozens of shopping channels selling everything from wigs to discount jewelry to Samurai steak knives sharp enough to slice open a can of peaches. I had to open the motel door to check where I was.

The night was cold and full of stars. The truck was gone. The motel office windows were dark. There was just my car and the green Vacancy sign at the entrance to the parking lot. I was in the middle of nowhere, as the saying goes. In the quiet of the night the face of a used-car salesman wearing an absurd toupee kept returning, as did the squealing and clapping contestants in some game show.

Anyone who asks about American identity has to contend with its huge empty spaces and whatever this other thing is that the multichannel TV brought me. That mind-boggling, absurd, and exhilarating aspect of America where one finds oneself watching a French Revolution costume drama in Japanese is familiar to Steinberg. American identity was always about having many identities, about having a permanent identity crisis, about attempting to invent oneself over and over again.

American towns in Steinberg's drawings are like movie sets for a horse opera. A bank, a barbershop, a hotel, a clothing store or two, and a saloon, as you expect to find. A few cars are parked along the short stretch of pavement, but no pedestrians are in view. The buildings are either all identical or, more likely, each built in a different architectural style. Nothing for anyone to do there but spend days scratching their heads in wonder.

In bigger towns, that jumble of styles is even worse. America, Steinberg discovered, is the place where the cultural history of the world holds its garage sale. Here it is not unusual to find a Renaissance madonna hanging in a provincial museum outside of which there's a strip of gas stations, motels, burger heavens, and Pizza Huts. In San Francisco, I once saw a small Buddha in a window of a dry-cleaning store chaperoning a wedding dress and a tuxedo. Every cultural artifact, every variation of style can be encountered here in oddest company. Only in America can Don Quixote be found charging the Egyptian pyramids, as he does in a Steinberg drawing.

> He who has not felt the difficulties of his art does nothing
> that counts.
>
> —Chardin

To make himself an original, an artist usually tends to refine one technique, pursue one idea of painting, leaving out all the other options available. Picasso is an exception to that, and so is Steinberg. His originality has meant inclusiveness. For him all art of the past is still contemporaneous, its ways of image making still valid. At times a Steinberg drawing can be like an Ellis Island of art styles. Classic, Romantic, baroque, mannerist, impressionist, expressionist, and cartoonish figures party together. Everything from naturalism to the more abstract, more geometric pole of representation is his concern. For him there's no privileged way of making images. Each style is point of view with its language and grammar. The principles of construction and expression of our disguises are the subject of his comic topology.

That, of course, is what makes him so difficult to classify. Born in Romania, educated in Italy, uprooted by Hitler and Stalin, not quite an American, no longer a European, he is an enigma even to himself. He has pictured himself variously as a blurred photograph on a badly stained passport, a thumbprint wearing a shirt and a tie, a yellowed, dog-eared birth certificate covered with illegible signatures, and as a seventy-year-old school picture with all of its faces equally indistinct and a blue arrow pointing to a face. In the manner of Pirandello, what we encounter in Steinberg's work are a thousand characters in search of their author.

For instance, he drew a lone man with an official rubber-stamp imprint in the sky above him. He drew the left hand drawing the right hand as the right hand drew the left hand at the same time. He drew another man with a pen crossing himself out. He drew a labyrinth and himself in it. He drew sixteen identical empty horizons. He drew many small indistinct figures identically dressed in black standing in groups or apart from each other in a vast landscape. He drew a man who when he spoke had a huge scribble come out of his mouth. He drew a Sisyphus pushing a boulder-sized question mark up the hill.

"Drawing is the probity of art," said Ingres. To draw a line is to draw a segment of one's autobiography. To draw is to ask, Where am I now? Where was I before? Where shall I be next? "The line is a living being with a mind of its own," Kandinsky told us. Of course. When the line was still a point, it was promised that if it stayed straight it had the option of going all the way to infinity. Well, yes, but . . . only by curving, only by going crooked, as it were, can a line be an individual and distinguish itself from other lines. In the meantime, to pass the time, it stages battles on a piece of paper with art and fate. Steinberg is a funambulist tiptoeing over the finest of all lines, that of being and time, a philosopher who draws.

The tragedian seeks what remains untouched by change; the comic spirit delights in metamorphosis. A comic vision is almost by definition Heraclitean. Everything, as in vaudeville and in silent comedies, is in constant flux. The tragic sense comes out of a profound disquiet with appearances; the comic loves the way the imagination can transform the world. Both are critical enterprises, revolts against human fate. What Steinberg does can be described as a comic inquiry into the myriad ways in which we represent ourselves.

"Everything that exists is an artist and is engaged in refining its appearance," he has said. Everywhere we look, the imagination has been at work. As he makes us see the many ways in which we create idealized pictures of ourselves, he makes us laugh. It's all about disguises, finally. There's a costume party always going on, as the realists fail to notice. One comes away from Steinberg's work convinced that only laughter can grasp the essence of this mad century.

He has a drawing, for instance, called "Ship of State." Science, Peace, Freedom, Law, Order, Uncle Sam, Lady Liberty, and the representatives of the two political parties dressed as baseball players ride in it. In the water, a mermaid whose bust is marked FUN and whose submerged fish-tail is marked PROFIT, swims around this ship of fools.

One feels in much of Steinberg's work both the presence of deliberateness and spontaneity. In the debate between copying and inventing, he does both. He is a careful thinker whose drawing instrument has a mind of its own. Or perhaps, more accurately, it has a tongue in its cheek. While the mind ponders, the hand laughs.

In Steinberg the visual is never far from language. The adventures of words such as *Beauty, Truth, God,* and others are the subject of some of his drawings. The word *Help* falls off a pier. The word *Nobody* is thinking of *Nothing* while standing on the word *Nowhere.* In the fairgrounds, the booth and shooting galleries are called Mondrian, Rimbaud, Rasputin, Kierkegaard, *Fear and Trembling.* In another drawing, a fat man with a bow and arrow is shooting at a speech balloon full of ornate and illegible writing.

It's the staggering variety, the seemingly endless range of invention of his many drawings that astonishes.

A man has wheels on his feet and an opening on his back with a ladder down which ten of his exact replicas are descending. A small dog sits on a carpet that has a lion embroidered on it. An old man raises a doll-like little girl to get a closer look at the moon. A small boy is being scolded by his mother for cutting off the peacock's tail with a pair of scissors. Uncle Sam is the matador: He's waving an American flag in front of a huge Thanksgiving turkey, and we laugh.

In towns with cowboy movie names, driving past churches advertising bingo nights, miniature-golf courses, trailer parks, fried chicken roadstands, and automobile graveyards, Steinberg's Don Quixote charging a huge pineapple comes to mind. Only he, among the contemporary artists and writers, saw this hodgepodge of the exotic and ordinary for what it is: a fool's paradise, but one worthy of great art, an art that demands a "genuine clumsiness," as he himself has remarked in describing the qualities of a good drawing.

Over a lifetime of drawing, Steinberg has given us a body of work that reminds me of Walt Whitman's *Leaves of Grass* in its epic sweep, except for the laughter. Steinberg's vast inventory of the American dream is our first comic epic. Suspicious of all ideological and aesthetic systems, his work is a gargantuan defense of laughter against every variety of utopia and accompanying dogma, including that of art.

Holly Wright's Photographs of Hands

> the power of the visible
> is the invisible
>
> —Marianne Moore

The philosophers and the mystics have told us again and again: the key to the mysteries is already in our hands. It was always there. We only have to open our hand, finger by finger, and find it.

"He looked at his hands without recognizing them," we say of the murderer.

If to our eyes both of our hands appear to be empty, it's because we haven't looked well enough. The palm readers know better. The darkest place, according to the Chinese proverb, is always underneath the lamp. The crisscrossed, broken, and faded lines of the secret map of our lives lie in our open hand.

The magician and the card trickster who practice sleight of hand know we do not always trust our eyes. At the very moment they are rolling up their sleeves and showing us that their hands are not concealing anything from us, an egg or an ace of spades makes its miraculous appearance between their fingers.

What things seem to be and what they truly are is the perennial subject of philosophical inquiry. The play of ambiguities they generate is also the concern of all arts. If we were not all natu-

From the *Yale Review* 84, no. 4 (1996): 26–37.

rally curious as to the difference between the two, neither magic nor photography would be possible.

Surprise me, we ask the artist. Make the familiar strange again. Restore wonder to our lives. It's not the truth we crave, but a new visual experience. Without its obsession with new image, modern painting and poetry would be unimaginable.

We do not identify at first the hands in Wright's photographs, of course. For all we know, we could be looking at Indian (Tantric) sculptures with their seemingly infinite variety of sexual embraces. That's how exotic these familiar hands have become.

Wright offers us a new kind of trompe l'oeil. Her photographs are mirrors, but of a strange kind. We can see ourselves reflected in them only if we close our eyes. These may be the hands we clasp behind our head while our eyes are veiled in reverie.

Where does the image in the photograph come from, we ask ourselves? Is it inside my head? Is it in the photograph itself? We are looking at Wright's hands with our eyes simultaneously open and shut.

How is that possible, you ask?

Look at the photographs and you'll know what I mean.

Secret nooks and crannies of the body and images of making love float out of the dark into the milky light in the back of our heads. It's a shock. Wright's photographs are unquestionably erotic, and that, we must remember, is an experience unknown to the aesthetic and moral tradition in this country. That, in my mind, is precisely what makes them so delightful and so subversive.

Photography is an art that plays off darkness against light, the visible against the hidden in the same way that eroticism does. Can we say that any image blurred and difficult to identify becomes charged erotically? Pornography shows everything; eroticism gives us only a peek through the keyhole of our parents' bedroom.

Memory, imagination, and desire grasp the offered hand, as it were. The figure of speech applicable here would be synecdoche: a part stands for the whole. Perhaps all acts of imagination are a search for the absent phantom of our desire?

Here, for instance, is an index finger sticking up with sugar on it. "Powdered sugar, the white gold of candy and pastry makers," Piero Camporesi says. The fine arts, we might say, are poetry, painting, music, reverie, and the licking of sticky fingers.

Our first toys were our hands. Our first taste of home cooking was sucking our fingers in the crib. When you love something, we learned then, it's best to use the tongue, and even better to put it in your mouth.

Two fingers smeared with what might be crème fraîche. The highest compliment you can pay to a cook:

"It was so good, we wanted to lick our fingers."

Our mothers knew, the hand that finds its way into a honey jar will stray under someone's skirt or into someone's pants sooner or later.

"The flies in the temple imitate the hands of the people with prayer beads," says the Japanese poet Issa.

Of course, we think. Our dogs and cats and even the flies on our walls are watching our hands day and night.

The hand and its five fingers: the continuous live sex show in the theater of Mr. and Mrs. Anybody.

Only a good photographer would see the hands for what they really are.

Open Wounds

Two books of photographs of the war in the former Yugoslavia, and specifically the siege of Sarajevo and Mostar from the summer of 1992 to September 1993. We see sniper victims lying in the streets, people with arms and legs blown off, corpses wrapped in plastic, wrecked churches and mosques, crowds of refugees on the run, young soldiers proudly wielding their weapons, children playing among the ruins or selling cigarettes. Every window is broken, every street strewn with rubble. After every photograph one reaches the inescapable conclusion that what one is looking at is the massacre of the innocent, the triumph of evil and stupidity.

The camera is the eyewitness. "Looking at a photograph, I inevitably include in my scrutiny the thought of that instant, however brief, in which a real thing happened to be motionless in front of the eye," writes Roland Barthes. This is the power of a documentary photograph. One sits at the breakfast table sipping coffee and turning the pages of the daily newspaper only to come to a photograph of a child killed in the street, lying in a pool of blood. Look and see, the photograph tells us, this really happened. The image is far more convincing than the word. Seeing the dead piled up like lumber to be bulldozed in concentration camps liberated by the allies at the end of World War II made the unthinkable suddenly believable.

The photograph tells the truth, we think. Still, one needs to be reminded here that pictures of atrocities were used and

Review of *Farewell to Bosnia,* photographs by Gilles Peress; *God Be with You: War in Croatia and Bosnia-Herzegovina,* photographs by Martin A. Sugarman.

continue to be used by the media on all sides in former Yugoslavia to fan the flames of hatred and enrage the various ethnic groups against each other. The rule of the propagandist is: you must never show what we did, but only what the other side did to us. The books under review, for instance, do not show any Serbian dead. Consequently, one cannot look through these photographs without ending by feeling a murderous loathing for the Serbs.

Then there is the question of voyeurism. Who hasn't felt ashamed by one's own curiosity in turning the pages of such books? Many of these photographs of atrocities are beautiful as photographs. One finds oneself admiring the godlike man with the camera who sought not only to document the horror, but also managed to catch the aesthetic side of the human drama. There is no such thing as an innocent eye, of course. One frames only a part of what one sees. Inevitably, one always makes choices. It takes skill to make a powerful image that "imparts humanity to the inhuman world," as Clarence John Laughlin said. It is the "art" in the photograph that makes the image stick in our minds.

Gilles Peress's book has more than two hundred uncaptioned photographs. Most of them are taken in a hurry, many from moving vehicles. We don't know where we are and what the people are running from precisely. Peress is very good at photographing crowds, conveying the panic and bewilderment of the innocent caught between two sides.

"Suffering people look the same everywhere," a friend of mine said, turning the pages of this book. It's true. A face contorted with pain or sobs is the same face the world over. What one remembers are the images that individualize the faces in the crowd, images where there is a clear sense of one life, one moment, one human being's tragic fate.

A man is pushing his grandmother in a wheelbarrow. The family photo album lies open on the floor of a gutted house outside of which the fruit trees are in bloom. It's springtime. The walls in the city are covered with obituary notices. A child with eyes bandaged is being led down a busy street by his mother. In one of the most powerful images in Peress's book, a man in the morgue approaches three stretchers with bodies lying on the floor and, recognizing a friend or relative, covers his face. In the next photograph the same man is turning away with his face still covered. The morgue attendant is expressionless as he stands watching him. He has seen all this before.

Sugarman's photographs are more carefully taken. His book is less the work of a journalist, more the work of a portrait artist. People pause for him. His photographs are identified and captioned. He has a feel for the monumental. The clouds and the dark sky above the ruins give his images a literary quality. I was reminded of Isaac Babel's stories of the Russian Revolution, the way he juxtaposes lyrical images of nature with horrors of the war: "Fields flowered around us, crimson with poppies. . . . lying on his back was an old man, a dead old man. His throat had been torn out and his face cleft in two," writes Babel.

There are some truly fine photographs in Sugarman's book: An old man with a cane and a shopping bag all alone crossing a street in Sarajevo. Three mad women holding each other in some unidentified hospital. A new apartment building with all its windows broken. A naked young woman raped and killed. A handsome, very young soldier observing a burial in Sarajevo. A street vendor selling brooms outside some ruins. People squatting under umbrellas at the cemetery during sniper fire; the four coffins lying on the ground unattended.

Only the young soldiers and the children are smiling in both books. This corresponds to my own memories of World War II in Yugoslavia. I was eight years old when the war ended and remember being terribly unhappy that I now had to go to school instead of roaming the streets with my buddies and having fun. As for the soldiers in our neighborhood, we'd sit at their feet listening to their adventures with fascination and envy. That's probably one reason why nobody ever learns anything from history in that unhappy country.

Assembly Required

The poet is like a compulsive talker at a funeral. People nudge him and tell him to be quiet and he apologizes, agrees that this is not the place, and so on and so forth as he goes on blabbering.

Cioran writes, "God is afraid of man . . . . man is a monster, and history has proved it."

My ideal is Robert Burton's *The Anatomy of Melancholy,* a catalog of many varieties of mopiness human beings are subject to, everything from the gloom caused by the evils of the world to the kind caused by lover's squabbles. Burton, who is one of the great stylists in the language, wrote the book to relieve his own low spirits. The result is the most cheerful book on general unhappiness we have.

"A book suitable for reading in an abandoned house among weeds on a still night and a full stomach," writes Felisberto Hernandez, who once described a young woman about to recite one of her poems as assuming an attitude that made one think of something between infinity and a sneeze.

In no other century, in no other literature of the past has the image been this important. In the age of ideology and advertisement, the poet, too, trusts the eyes more than the ear.

No preconceived aesthetic sense can guide the poet and the artist in American cities, where chance rules.

From *Field* (forthcoming).

In poetry, to quote a bluesman who calls himself Satan, one must "learn to do wrong with respect."

The soul squawking to the body about its days being numbered. That's what most blues songs and lyric poems are about.

Collage is a mystic's medium.

I'm a jailbird from every Garden of Eden, every utopia that has ever been imagined.

"The future will be post-individualist," the critic Frederic Jameson tells us. Whether it'll be Stalin's, Hitler's, or Mao's model, he doesn't say.

I'm preparing to relocate to a rock in the sea.

Things, do you know suffering? The mystery of the object is the mystery of a closed door. The object is the place where the real and the imaginary collide.

Ars poetica: I ate the white chickens and left the red wheelbarrow out in the rain.

As a poet, the Lord of the Universe is hopelessly obscure.

Intense experience eludes language. Language is the Fall from the awe and consciousness of being.

To be a poet is to feel something like a unicyclist in a desert, a pornographic magician performing in the corner of the church during Mass, a drag queen attending night classes and blowing kisses at the teacher.

The prose poem is a fabulous beast like the sphinx. A monster made up of prose and poetry.

A horror movie for vegetarians: Greasy sausages kept falling from the sky into people's bean soup.

"They are bad for you," my friends tell me. As if all that stands between me and immortality are a couple of Italian sausages.

She is a passionate multiculturalist except when it comes to ethnic food. This is where she draws the line. If these minorities could learn to forgo deep-fried foods, she could open her heart to them even more.

In the school of virtue, I'm still five years old. I want to sit in some woman's lap and suck her breast, but they won't let me. Give me my thumb to chew at least, I protest! But they sprinkle hot chili sauce on all my fingers and order me to stand in the corner.

American unhappiness has no history because history has to do with real events and not with a Dream.

How is it that certain expressions of our own subjectivity in poetry strike the reader as merely self-indulgent or sentimental, while other, equally personal, have a universal resonance? The answer may be that there are two kinds of poets: Those who ask the reader to wallow in self-pity with them and those who simply remind them of their common human predicament.

To rescue the banal is every lyric poet's ambition.

All lives are strange, but the lives of immigrants and exiles are even more so. My parents died a long way from where they were born. It's not how they imagined their lives were going to be. Even at the age of eighty-eight in a nursing home in Dover, New Hampshire, my mother was puzzled. What does it all mean, she wanted to know? What terrified her was the likelihood that it meant nothing.

Our conservatives and liberals both dream of censorship. Their ideal, without them realizing it, is Mao's China. Only a few books in bookstores and libraries, and every one of them carrying a wholesome message.

American academics suffer from cultural insecurity. They really don't know who they are, but our writers do, and that's the problem.

"She faked orgasm each time she masturbated," writes an unknown wit in a tabloid.

My father's comment on an old waiter in our favorite Greek restaurant: "His grandpa ran the shadow projector in Plato's Cave."

"I would have given my pants for . . . ," he kept shouting all his life.

Some readers find my poems obscure because, well, I don't sum it up for them. That is to say, I have too much respect for them to play the preacher, but that's what they want from their poets.

My student Jeff McRae says, "Life at its best is a beautiful sadness."

To me the test of a literary theory is what it has to say about the lyric poem. If it avoids the lyric or stumbles over it, I say forget it. It's a fraud.

Here's the first rule of insomnia: Don't talk to the heroes and villains on the screen.

Memory: Not my own. Whose then? At 4 A.M., when the heart skips a beat or two, I saw myself with arms spread on the gallows about to address a huge crowd and found no words in my mouth.

Years later, when some of my high school teachers in Yugoslavia were told that I had graduated from the university, they just laughed and refused to believe any of it.
    "That lazy bum? Never in a thousand years."
    My mother took an equally dim view.
    "He'll end up in prison," she told everybody.
    I don't think she ever truly believed I was actually a professor

at a university. He's lying to me, she thought, or he has them all hoodwinked in some way, but is bound to be found out sooner or later.

In the beginning there were Whitman and Dickinson and Poe. Whitman was our Homer and Dickinson our Sappho, but who the hell was Poe?

The aim of ideologies of ethnicity, nationality, religion, and gender is to remove the sense of one's own individual limitations and failure as a human being and to replace the "I" by a "we."

The best recommendation for wine, tobacco, sex, and loose talk is that every so-called moral majority is against them.

The often heard assertion that there's no truth outside of language is just jive.

Our rich are torn between self-pity (they're paying too much in taxes) and self-adulation. To live without excuses is now a profoundly un-American attitude.

He kissed ass so much his brain had turdified.

Even birds detest poetry, it seems. The beauty of the sunset over the quiet lake made them holler. Even the leaves, shushing each other into sleep, grew agitated. The grandeur of the sky lasted just as long as it took them to make their complaints, and then they were done.

The identification of what remains untouched by change has been the philosopher's task. Art and literature, on the contrary, have been delighted with the ephemeral—the smell of bread, for instance.

Centuries ago, when the king's advisers and seers gave wrong predictions as to the outcome of military campaigns, they were tortured and publicly executed. In our days, they continue being called "experts" and appear on TV.

Deterrence by example. Let's bomb X so that Y and Z will realize we mean business and behave. By that logic, why not hang a few crooked politicians and bankers so that others may be warned?

Always the foreigner, the stranger, someone a bit fishy. Even the smiling dummies in store windows eyed me with suspicion today.

Rubbing against so many strangers in so many places and aping their ways to pass for a native has made you incomprehensible even to yourself.

"We lost everything," my mother used to say. She was right. Everything we ever had in terms of possessions and identities was no more. One day we were folks next door and the next we were riffraff without a country.

Nietzsche: "That the lie is permitted as means to pious ends is a part of the theory of every priesthood."

American writers have been lucky that the rich and powerful have had no interest in making them their concubines. Our so-called intellectuals have not been so fortunate.

The unbelievers say with the scientists that the morning light has no consciousness; the believers know it does.

Orphan factories and scapegoat farms are the Balkans' chief economy.

Wary of every enthusiasm, ready to run away at the first opportunity. Only on the subject of the absolute scumminess of politicians do I feel completely confident.

At night frequently I have the same dream: A border guard steps with his boot on my passport.

How to kill a lot of people and sleep like a baby continues to be the statesman's ideal. That's why he needs intellectuals to divide murderers into good and bad, to explain that we are doing evil to these people for their own good. Brutality and violence always require a new, superior morality.

Nationalism is the love of the smell of our collective shit.

Any ideology or belief that doesn't have hatred as spice has no chance of becoming popular. To be a true believer you have to be a champion hater.

Here's my contribution to the politics of nostalgia: The servants of the rich (our politicians and journalists) should wear doorman's uniforms. Let flunkies be instantly recognized from the distance, as in the old days.

The silent laughing chorus behind all ideas of progress.

Every poetic image asks why is there something rather than nothing, as it renews our astonishment that things exist.

There's a tradition of wonderful misfits in literature, unclassifiable writers and poets, like Michaux and Edson, suspicious of literature, who are at the same time its biggest addicts. Only a style that is a carnival of styles seems to please them. A poetry, in short, that has the feel of the circus, a sideshow, vaudeville, facts stranger than fiction, fake miracles and superstitions, dreambooks sold at supermarket counters, etc.

I never "write." I just tinker.

The prose poem is like a dog that talks.

It is possible to make astonishingly tasty dishes from the simplest ingredients. That's my aesthetics. I'm the poet of the frying pan and my love's little toes.

To preserve the standpoint of the individual is the continuous struggle. The tribe is always trying to reform you, teach you some manners and a new vocabulary.

For any conspiracy theory history is a sham. Every public event is a guise behind which true events take place. Conspiracy, in that sense, is a theory of representation. What you see is really not what is truly there.

Free will is an illusion. In conspiracy theory, the law of gravity is absolute. Planes cannot fly.

The world is always old. There are no new events because conspiracy is eternal.

Conspiracy is the only true theology. All other theologies are part of the great conspiracy.

You think all this is funny? Your laughter, Simic, is a sign of foolishness. You're a dupe, a gullible hayseed when it comes to the dark forces of conspiracy playing all around you.

Wittgenstein Bubble Gum: Trying to say that which cannot be said. Endeavoring, exerting myself daily—and how!—to woo, to throw a net over, to grapple and scuffle with that which cannot be voiced, intoned, ventriloquized as to its content, even in a ghastly stammer, and is, perhaps, given only in small hints by a hand gesture, a shrugged shoulder, a long sigh. Humdinger! Language is a monkey wrench.

American identity is really about having many identities simultaneously. We came to America to escape our old identities, which the multiculturalists now wish to restore to us.

The muses are cooks. Poetry is a kind of cookery. I divide my poems between appetizers, stews, and desserts.

On the invisible line between sayable and the unsayable—the lyric poem.

If music is about the use of time and painting about the use of space, in lyric poems they're brought together. Image brings space into language (time), which the language then fragments into space.

Poetry like the movies worries about sequence, framing, montage, and cutting.

Not all innocent victims qualify as innocents, I've concluded, reading the daily papers for the last forty years. The ethnic group has first to become fashionable as an object of pity before their innocence as victims is accepted. Otherwise, forget it.

Stupidity is having a national revival. All you need to do is turn on the TV to see its big, friendly smile.

A fierce competition is in progress as to who is the biggest victim among us. Right now, the children of privilege are winning and the poor and the unlettered are losing. Money buys even victimhood.

A poem like a holy icon, painted in secret hope that some day a god may come to inhabit it miraculously.

Didn't Joyce call poetry "soul butter" somewhere?

I miss phrenology. It would be nice to have someone feel the bumps on the heads of our presidential candidates while they address the nation.

Ambrose Bierce: "That immortal ass, the average man."

It's getting dark and I'm showing my teeth to the hell hound running behind me on the road to nowhere.

Soon we'll all be returning to Emily Dickinson's dark closet. Funambulist of the invisible, make it quick, start your walk.

Night Sky

To Linda Connor

This Saturday night, the sky is a great Pythagorean jukebox
sparkling in a corner of a darkened night club.

> The black wax is spinning.
> Tarantula nebula.
> It's one of the golden oldies.
> The mystics among us will hear the music.

Written for *On the Music of the Spheres,* a limited edition book of Linda
Connor's photographs of the night sky and published by Whitney Mu-
seum in 1996.

The star map hanging down over the blackboard in my grade school classroom remains where it was forty-seven years ago. The trees are bare and it's still raining. Everyone is bent over their work and I alone am daydreaming while watching a small insect crawl over the map on its way to the Dog Star.

He wants to be one of its fleas is what I think.

A large family of circus performers. There go the bear and the lion who sheds golden tears. The carrot-haired Venus and the winged-horse Pegasus come next. The show has started. There are dwarfs, too, I'm told. The acrobats and the fire-eaters have sequins sewn to their black suits.

How do we win the love of Betelgeuse? The trumpets, the drums, and the voice of the master of ceremonies are much too far away.

Even the encyclopedia entry about the sky is full of poetry:

"During spring evenings," it says, "Orion is still above the horizon; Leo is high up with Virgo to the East; Capella is descending in the northwest and Vega is rising in the northeast. In the west, Aldebaran and the Pleiades are still visible."

And—I want to write in the margin: There goes my grandmother, the one the neighbors call the witch, riding a white goat while clutching the Holy Bible to her breast.

The cow alone in the fields, does it raise its heavy head to gaze at the stars?

How about daddy longlegs, the pair of fireflies, the lone cricket?

The night sky loves only the solitary ones. To the one sitting in a corner with his face to the wall, it offers its own secret invitation on the breath of night wind.

When he finds himself in the desert or on the mountaintop, he will want immediately to confide himself to the sky.

Oh the things we would all say to the stars in the sky if we found ourselves alone in a lifeboat at sea.

It's the Death Mask of the Universe we are staring at.

There are candles burning in its eye-pits and in its huge gaping mouth.

Where is the ear, dark as the bottom of a coffee cup, where all our prayers went in?

Where's the other ear where they all went out?

> Where am I? That's my first question.
> —Samuel Becket, *The Unnameable*

I'm nothing; a mere drop in the ocean.

My existence is a matter of complete indifference to you, Cassiopeia.

Cities burning, empires falling, someone addressing the crowd from the gallows with a noose already around his neck are all equally of no importance to you.

Perhaps the ecstasy of hearing your beautiful name on our lips is all that you know?

And then, more likely, you don't even know about that.

If the photographers are soul-thieves, whose soul is being stolen in a photograph of the night sky?

The soul of the last one to go to bed and the soul of the first one to rise in the morning, perhaps?

Photography is a black art like alchemy. It turns matter into spirit and spirit into matter.

Still, there are moments when looking at a photograph of a night sky we have a hunch what the word *soul* means, what the word *infinity* encompasses.

And then, friends, there are those clear summer nights when Time, our killer, goes to take a long siesta in the star-strewn meadows.

The old clock on the wall that ticks even more loudly after midnight, because its two hands are afraid of each other in the dark, is quiet for once.

No one can find the key to wind it up.

If you want to know the correct time, look deep into the eyes of a black cat.

The ambition of Byzantine church architecture is to invite the sky in and make it welcome between the walls of the humblest of its churches. The interiors of their domes, therefore, resemble a planetarium. The holy icon of the Mother of God here below is like a saucer of milk set out for the stars in the sky to drink at midnight.

The heaven in Byzantine frescoes has the appearance and the smell of a burning candle about to be put out by the galactic wind.

The levitating archangels and saints have the awestruck faces of children riding a Ferris wheel.

The lazy light of the stars is trying to calm our jitters.

Hush, it says, the moment the night falls.

In my lifelong insomnia, I even tried counting Greek and Egyptian gods like sheep.

Psst, I told them, when their stone-steps in the sky got to be too loud.

After taking a good look at the sky through a telescope at the planetarium, my mother concluded, "The whole creation is an absurdity! A practical joke."

Large numbers gave her a headache. For her, the commonplace claim that the universe is infinite was a comic rather than a tragic proposition.

I, too, rejoice in the craziness of it all. For me, the sky full of stars is the unbeliever's paradise.

> I was put under a spell one night on a high hill.
> —Guillaume IX of Aquitaine

No sooner had I started my reverie than I was light-years from the earth, a tightrope walker on his way to the confetti palace.

I was the galactic Marco Polo.

I rode a unicycle with its wheel on fire.

I saw the stars go down to catch a brief glimpse of themselves in lakes and rivers.

The solitude of the timeless sparkling in the deep black water.

If not for the dog barking after me tonight, none of us would know we were here.

My private interview with the Infinite Universe went something like this:

So, this is the brightly lit gambling casino of the imagination?

The bets are constantly being made and the roulette wheels, as far as I can see, turn unattended?

(Did I imagine it, or did it really shrug its shoulders in reply?)

A worldwide chain of firecracker supply stores is what this is.

The owner wears a black cape and has a huge black moustache like a famous hypnotist.

His daughters are writing secret love notes in Arabic script to a mysterious someone.

"Call me in the evening," one note says.

Love: the volume of one of the distant radio galaxies turned down real, real low.

Contributor's Note

I pleaded with my Death to at least allow me to nibble my pencil while he took bites of me. He kindly let me have a sheet of paper and an eraser too.

My lifelong subject, despite appearances to the contrary, was always an unknown woman who made me forget my name every time we bumped into each other on the street.

—Who am I, I asked my Death, but he just licked his fingers in reply.

The unknown woman wasn't any more forthcoming. She paid me no mind whatsoever, even though I was often sprawled before her on the sidewalk like an old dog overcome with memories of happier days.

Once at the bus stop, she asked me for the time in a voice that promised a life of bliss. I blurted out something about my Death, how he's even found me a publisher, but she was no longer listening.

It had started to rain. Everybody ran for cover. I did too. We watched her take off her high-heel shoes and pull down her panty hose. Then she marched through the puddles, head thrown back, arms spread wide as if she were about to fly.

I wanted to join her, but I hesitated, and then the torrential rain blurred the sight of her and made her vanish forever.

UNDER DISCUSSION
David Lehman, General Editor
Donald Hall, Founding Editor

Volumes in the Under Discussion series collect reviews and essays about individual poets. The series is concerned with contemporary American and English poets about whom the consensus has not yet been formed and the final vote has not been taken. Titles in the series include: